SPIRIT

PASSION

give

ocean

INSPIRE

learn

Love

JOY

DES

CREATE

TRUTH

REST

the home
SPA

the home SPA

creating a personal sanctuary

Carol Endler Sterbenz

with Genevieve A. Sterbenz

**Andrews McMeel
Publishing**

Kansas City

99 00 01 02 03 TWP 10 9 8 7 6 5 4 3 2 1

Sterbenz, Carol Endler.
   The home spa : creating a personal sanctuary / Carol Endler
  Sterbenz, Genevieve Sterbenz.
     p.   cm.
   Includes bibliographical references and index.
   ISBN 0-7407-0052-9 (hardcover)
   1. Beauty, Personal. 2. Women--Health and hygiene. 3. Spa pools-
-Health aspects.   I. Sterbenz, Genevieve. II. Title.
  RA778.S815 1999
  646.7'042--dc21   99-26700
                                                      CIP

Every effort has been made to present the information in this book in a clear, complete, and accurate manner. It is important that all instructions are followed carefully, as failure to do so could result in injury. The authors, and editors and publisher or Andrews McMeel disclaim any and all liability resulting therefrom.

READ THIS FIRST: IMPORTANT HEALTH WARNINGS

Essential oils are potent and should be treated and stored like any other medicine. They should be kept out of the reach of children. If you are pregnant, and in your first trimester, avoid all essential oils. Thereafter, pregnant women and the elderly should consult a doctor before using them.

In all cases, essential oil should be used with the following cautions:

Always Dilute: Never use essential oils full-strength as they can cause burning and irritation to the skin. Avoid mucous membranes and eye areas. Always dilute essential oil in a carrying agent like a base oil or water and mix them in a safe proportion as directed in the specific recipes.

Do a Skin Patch Test: Before using essential oils, be sure to do a patch test, especially if you have sensitive skin or are prone to allergies. Blend together 5 drops of the essential oil and ½ ounce of base oil. Dab a little of this mixture on the inside of your elbow or the back of your neck. Wait twelve hours. If redness or itching occurs, dilute further, or change to another essential oil, then repeat the patch test. *Cinnamon, clove, dwarf pine, oregano, savory, spearmint and thyme are known skin irritants even with dilution.*

Avoid the Sun: Certain essential oils cause photosensitivity. Avoid *bergamot, cold-pressed lime, neroli, lemon and grapefruit oil* for at least 12 hours before exposure to the sun.

Never Take Internally: Do not ingest essential oils. As few as a couple of drops can be toxic.

ATTENTION: SCHOOLS AND BUSINESSES
Andrews McMeel books are available at quantity discounts with bulk purchase for education, business, or sales promotional use. For information, please write to: Special Sales Department, Andrews McMeel Publishing, 4520 Main Street, Kansas City, Missouri 64111.

Acknowledgments

An interior is the

natural projection

of the soul.

—Coco Chanel

NO WORK OF THIS MAGNITUDE is ever accomplished without the talent and support of many people. We want to give our heartfelt thanks to:

Richard Felber whose extraordinary talent and vision are seen so clearly in the beautiful photographs; and his able and good spirited assistant, John Dee.

The homeowners who opened their doors to us, especially Michael Stanley, of Michael Stanley Antiques in Putnam CT, whose hospitality and generosity were beyond measure, and whose extraordinary collection of antiques were unselfishly loaned; and Andrew J. Schmitz III, Diane Galtieri and Terry Gregory who were willing to entertain our invasion.

The friends at Léron, who loaned the exquisite linen and towels, Frank and James at The Potted Palm in Providence, RI, who braved a snow storm to deliver Spring in all its glory, at The White Horse Inn in Putnam, CT for the silk roses; Linda Jines, of Sweet Cakes Soap Making Supplies, for the fragrance oils and invaluable guidance; Roberta Frauwirth who illustrated the patterns; and especially, Adrienne Johnson who was there in more ways than we can mention.

The staff at Andrews McMeel, who shepherded and shaped the work with sensitivity and knowing, especially our editor, Jean Lowe; Design Director, Stephanie R. Farley together with Lisa Martin and Becky Kanning; and Elizabeth Nuelle and Marti Petty in Production.

And last but not least, thank you to our wonderful family who surrounds us with love and humor.

Dedication

For my loving mother,

who made spirit

a matter of life

—Carol Endler Sterbenz

For L.K.A. and R.A.K.,

thank you for all your

love and support

—Genevieve A. Sterbenz

Table of contents

Introduction

We were sent into the world to live to the full

everything that awakens within us and everything that comes towards us.

Real divinity has a passionate instinct for creativity

and the fully inhabited life—

the greatest sin of all is the unlived life.

—John O'Donohue

IF WE ARE TO CREATE authentic and joyful lives, we must find ways to restore the intimate

connections we have to ourselves, in both body and spirit. In a world that puts demands on

our most precious inner resources and that strains the access we have to our own unique

voice, we can lose touch with the central guidance system that determines the sacredness

of the choices we make, the soul.

The Home Spa: Creating a Personal Sanctuary provides means to forge those crucial

connections to ourselves by suggesting ways to set up a supportive environment in our

home and to restore us through personal care rituals that confer all the benefits of a trip to

a spa—tranquillity and relaxation.

To create a haven for ourselves, we must plan. We must be determined to make a

x

place that is peaceful, intimate, and personal. Through our creative expression, we can make

this environment in our bathroom, either filled with or accented by simple things that we

have made ourselves. We can also gather objects we love, objects that hold the spirit of our

lives, and set them around us, with us at the epicenter of this sacred altar that is our home.

The Home Spa is a collection of ideas, a confluence of actual projects and inspirational

words, to guide you in creating a personal sanctuary. You can adapt any of the ideas in

this collection to your own tastes and needs. Whether your bathroom is modern or

vintage, whether it is large enough to hold stuffed chairs and a fully working fireplace

or is simply a small room, monastic in detail except for the trio of tub, sink, and toilet, its

fundamental essence is the same: to provide you with a private space in which to take care of yourself. You need only water and spirit, and the space will be transformed into your personal retreat.

For, regardless of the opulence or simplicity of your room, and independent of its style, you can turn a faucet and hear the gush of water as it leaves a spout and fills your tub. You can breathe in the aromatic herbal essences that ride on the vapor of hot water. You can relinquish your hold on the outside world, heed the primal call of water, and, in your own good company, take care of yourself.

And when you do, *be* there. Don't rush. Provide for the time you need in your retreat. Plan ahead for your rituals and allow your life during those rituals to be pared down to only your senses. When you do you will be able to achieve one of life's pure and satisfying pleasures, the timelessness of reposing in a bathtub resplendent with fragrant herbs, thick towels at the ready.

The Home Spa is here to lead you. With easy at-home ideas that appeal to the senses and take only a few seconds (stop and breathe in the fragrance of the potted herbs on the windowsill and ask yourself, What do I need right now?), projects that take a few minutes (combine grocery store ingredients to make a refreshing herbal splash), or ones

that take an hour or more (etch a beautiful design in a drinking glass designated for your

morning juice), this book can bring the gifts of connection and balance to your spirit, mind,

and body as it inspires you to turn off the phone, hang a Do Not Disturb sign on the door,

withdraw into the sanctuary of your inner thoughts, and reconnect to your holy self.

preparing your
personal sanctuary

We need time to dream, time to remember,

and time to reach the infinite. Time to be.

—Gladys Taber

YOU DO NOT have to renovate or redecorate your bathroom to create a personal sanctuary, but there are certain elements essential to establishing the soothing calm of a visit to a spa.

Gather the essentials you have—clean, thick towels, washcloths and loofahs, an absorbent bath mat, a comfortable robe, and a pair of slippers. Then look at your space to see that you have also collected items that support your bathing and personal care rituals.

First, think about the ways you can establish privacy and intimacy. A paneled screen can be a crucial furnishing in this regard. In an instant a screen can provide a sense of containment and safety. It can be used to enclose a tub without the claustrophobia of drawing a shower curtain. Or simply hang a Do Not Disturb sign on the outside doorknob to preserve your sovereignty.

As important as security and privacy are, setting a mood that inspires relaxation is also vital. While your room color and style have already been set by your choices of wall color, fixtures, and tile, there are other ways to transform your bathroom into a personal refuge.

Lighting is essential in creating just the right mood. Low light, especially the warm glow of candles, can soften the hard edges of everything around you and inspire you to focus inward. Scented candles will also provide aromatherapeutic benefits that can have a powerful effect on your mind and your emotions. Collect tapers and set them in the arms of a multi-tiered candelabrum, or simply surround the edge of the tub with glimmering votive candles that have a pleasing fragrance. Perhaps, position a few mirrors around the room to reflect light, or add a flattering lamp to your vanity area.

Light needn't be contrived to be beneficial. Do not ignore the refreshing and healthful effects of natural light. There is nothing as soothing or pleasurable as bathing in the ambient half-light of dawn. Or for an afternoon soak, if your room is so oriented, enjoy the sunlight as it streams through a frothy, patterned sheer curtain hung from a nearby window or across the shower rod you have transformed with sprigs of rosemary and eucalyptus. And, if it is possible, open the window wide and let the fresh air in. Fresh air can expand your spirit.

Equally powerful are the effects of surrounding yourself with fresh flowers and foliage. Their color and scent can quiet or raise the spirit, depending on the essential properties of the varieties you choose. Sprinkle rose petals in the bathwater. Place silver cups with herbs on a windowsill. Fill vases with armloads of

2

eucalyptus, or drape a languorous garland lush with roses around the tub or over the showerhead. Their natural fragrances will be emitted when plant materials are exposed to heat and moisture, and they will fill the room with soothing aromas.

To further support your retreat within, listen to music. Music is known to set up sound vibrations that affect the body. The harmonics of certain music cause our bodies to release the hormone ACTH, which can inspire a sense of well-being and happiness. Play the radio or your stereo, selecting symphonic music or recordings of tonal prayers and chants.

Contemplative and solitary, bathing can also include listening to the wise words of philosophers and teachers of today and the past. And because our spirits evolve at different rates at different periods in our lives, and according to the personal lessons we experience in our lifetimes, only we know what touches us. So consider listening to a meditation tape you have made yourself, one that relates to your personal beliefs and philosophies, or one that combines words and music that help you relax and get centered.

Finally, before you slip off your bathrobe and slide into the water, plan to move a low table, or even a chair, next to the tub. If you shower, set a pedestal table nearby. Fill the table with all the jars and bottles of creams, lotions, and scrubs you love, and any other items you need to pamper yourself. And, for instant access, straddle a bath caddy across the tub, piling it with amenities such as your favorite book of poetry and something refreshing to drink, like herbal tea or mineral water with a slice of lemon. Then, get ready to relax deeply and discover your sublime self, flowing like a secret stream of wisdom and just waiting to be discovered.

3

Striped privacy screen

ADMITTEDLY NOT calming, but oh so sleek and vigorous, this screen can simply satisfy your need for a little added energy in your sanctuary. The screen may look imposing, but it is deceivingly practical and versatile. With individual panels that move on hinges, it can be used in even moderately small bathrooms. You can fold up the screen partway to create a kind of accordion-pleat privacy panel, or you can stretch it out and form a wall. In addition, because the screen can be folded together to the width of one panel, it can be stored easily or moved to another room to create a private corner.

The screen is also appealing in other ways. The frame is sturdy and durable, and it is sensuous in detail. Gently curled finials break the linear rigidity. The panels have rods that stretch the fabric panels taut to prevent wrinkles. These rods are removable so that the fabric panels can be taken off and washed, or the fabric can be changed to coordinate with the seasons or the need for a quieter, more soothing print. This striped privacy screen coordinates with the Oversize Throw, page 9 and Bath Stool Cushion, pages 10-11.

materials

Wrought-iron screen with 3 removable panels

5⅓ yd. sturdy striped cotton fabric in black and white, 45 in. wide, or as desired

Matching thread

Optional

Six 4-inch tassels

3 embroidered emblems, 4½ in. high × 3½ in. wide, or as desired

You will also need: tape measure; pencil; scissors; straight pins; hand-sewing needle; fabric glue; sewing machine

directions

Note: Panels in the featured screen are stretched between metal rods that fit into notches at the top and bottom of each panel frame.

1 To calculate measurements for the panels on your screen, use a tape measure and pencil to measure and note the height and width of one panel opening.

2 Add 3 inches to height (A) for rod casings and ¾ inch to width (B) for side hems.

3 When buying fabric, use the measurements calculated in Steps 1 and 2 for each panel. *Note: For a three-panel screen, multiply by 3.*

4 Lay one cut panel, wrong side up, on a flat work surface.

5 Double-fold, pin, and machine-stitch ⅜-inch hems on the long sides of a panel, removing pins as you work; repeat for the remaining panels.

6 Lay a panel wrong side up on a flat work surface.

7 Double-fold and pin a ¾-inch hem at the top and bottom edges of a panel, top-stitching a scant ⅛ inch from the edge of the fold; repeat for the remaining panels.

8 To hang the panel, insert one rod from the screen into the top casing and reposition the rod in the screen.

9 Insert the second rod into the bottom casing of the panel, carefully pulling the panel taut and repositioning the rod at the bottom of the screen.

10 Repeat Steps 8 and 9 for the remaining panels.

5

Screen tassel

TASSELS ARE LITTLE works of art that can transform an ordinary accessory into something extraordinary. Whether suspended from a finial or attached to a bath wrap or cushion, tassels are elegant accents. But they can be quite expensive. Here is a quick guide to making your own.

materials

Skein heavy cotton yarn in color desired

You will also need: scrap cardboard; scissors; ruler; darning needle

directions

1
To make one tassel, cut a scrap of cardboard into a rectangle 8 inches high × 4 inches wide; fold the rectangle in half widthwise.

2
To form the body of the tassel, wrap the yarn sixty times around the height of the cardboard.

3
Slip the darning needle, threaded with 12 inches of yarn, under the skein at the folded edge of the cardboard, pulling the yarn to the midpoint.

4
Sew around the top of the skein 5 or 6 times to secure the tassel, tying the ends of the yarn in a double knot.

5
Cut through the yarn at the open end of the cardboard.

6
To make the head of the tassel, hold the skein at the tied end and wrap a 10-inch length of yarn around the top, beginning ¾ inch from the top knot.

7
To finish, knot the yarn and tuck the ends into the head.

8
Trim the fringe end of the tassel even.

Illustrated velvet pillow

IF YOU HAVE EVER done some of your foot care rituals without the support of a good stool or chair, you know how uncomfortable they can be when you are perched on the side of the tub or toilet. If your space is so small that you cannot fit a single piece of furniture inside your bathroom, make certain you have a lovely pillow nearby so that you can provide yourself a good seat.

materials

18-in.-square Poly-Fil pillow form

½ yd. cotton velvet, 36 in. wide

Matching thread

Optional

fabric square with iron-on transfer
    illustration (see page 26)

You will also need: hand-sewing needle; ruler; scissors; straight pins; sewing machine

directions

1
Cut the velvet in half lengthwise to yield two 18-inch squares.

2
Mark the seam lines on the wrong side of one square, ⅝ inch from the raw edges.

3
Optional: To attach an illustration to the cushion: Lay one velvet square on a flat working surface, nap side up; center the illustrated fabric square and topstitch around all four sides, a scant ¼ inch from the folded edges.

4
Lay the velvet squares together, right sides facing, naps facing the same direction, and raw edges even.

5
Machine-stitch the sides along the marked seam lines, leaving a 12-inch opening at the center of the last side for turning.

6
Clip the corners and turn the cover right side out.

7
Insert the pillow form and slip-stitch the opening closed.

7

Oversize throw

REGARDLESS OF THE STYLE of your bathroom, you can coordinate the cushion on your bath stool with several other accessories, especially the screen on page 4. Traditionally patterned fabrics can be used, of course, but for a change, consider mixing and matching low-pile animal prints. You can create a little electricity by matching a cushion in a zebra stripe with an embracing over-size bath throw. Animal prints are available in zebra, tiger, leopard, and cheetah. The fabric will be an invigorating surprise to your senses.

materials

4 yd. low-pile cotton in animal print,
    54 in. wide

Four 4-in.-long tassels

Matching thread

You will also need: tape measure; tailor's chalk; scissors; straight pins; sewing machine with heavy duty needle

directions

1 To prepare the front and back of the throw, lay the fabric horizontally on a flat work surface.

2 Measure, mark, and cut the fabric into two equal pieces, each measuring 72 × 54 inches.

3 To sew the throw, lay the pieces together, right sides facing, raw edges even.

4 Pin along the seam allowance around all four sides, ⅜ inch from the raw edge.

5 To position a tassel, insert the fringe end through the layers of fabric at one corner, pinning the end of the hanging cord between the layers; repeat with the three remaining tassels.

6 Machine-stitch around the sides of the throw, being careful to pivot around the corners and to sew through the tassel hanging cords, leaving 18 inches open in the middle of the last side for turning.

7 Clip the corners, then turn the throw right side out.

8 Slip-stitch the opening closed.

9 Press the seams flat, then topstitch around all four sides, 1 inch from the seam, setting the sewing machine at basting stitch.

9

Bath stool cushion

PERHAPS THE MOST PRACTICAL seating in any bathroom, regardless of size, is the stool. Lightweight, sturdy, and portable, stools are a real comfort to have around. They are even more comfortable when you add a thick cushion. This box-style cushion is customized to fit the seat of a wrought-iron stool. This bath stool cushion coordinates with the Striped Privacy Screen, page 4.

materials

Bath stool with 16-in.-square seat

16-in.-square foam cushion, 3 in. high

⅔ yd. low-pile cotton in animal print, 54 in. wide*

4 yd. brush fringe, 1 in. wide with plaited heading

1 yd. black grosgrain ribbon, ¾ in. wide

Matching thread

You will also need: butcher paper; pencil; ruler; tape; scissors; straight pins; sewing machine; hand-sewing needle

10

directions

Note: To custom-fit the cushion to your bath stool, make a butcher paper pattern of the seat area, adding ½ inch to each side for seam allowances. Make a second paper pattern for the box strip equal in length to the perimeter of the seat plus 1 inch* (this strip will need to be cut from two pieces of fabric) and equal in width to the height of the cushion plus 1 inch. Adjust the measurements of the foam cushion and fringe accordingly.

1
For seat sections, use your pattern to measure and cut two squares from the fabric.

2
For the box strip, measure and cut two strips of fabric, each with length equal to half the perimeter of the cushion plus 1 inch for seam allowance and width equal to the height of the cushion plus 1 inch for seam allowance.

3
Lay all the cut sections on a flat work surface wrong side up, and mark ½-inch seam lines on the sides of the square sections and along the tops and bottoms of the box strips.

4
To cut the length of fringe in half, apply tape to the midpoint at the plait, then cut through both tape and fringe.
Note: Do not remove the tape from the ends.

5
Position and pin the fringe all the way around one square seat section, beginning at the center of one side; overlap the taped ends.
Note: The plaited edge of the fringe should slightly overlap the raw edge of the fabric, fringe facing the center of the seat section.

6
Machine-stitch the fringe to the seat section ½ inch from the edge, pivoting around the corners and making certain the fringe does not get caught in the stitches; remove the tape.

7
Repeat Step 6 for the second seat section.

8
To prepare and attach the ties, cut the ribbon in four equal lengths.

9
Position and machine-stitch the midpoint of a ribbon to the midpoint of each corner of one seat section, ½ inch from the edge of the fringe.

10
To prepare the box strip, lay the sections together, right sides facing, raw edges even.

11
Machine-stitch the short sides, ½ inch from the raw edges, making one continuous fabric loop; press the seams flat.

12
Test-fit the loop box strip around the cushion, wrong side out.

13
Align the seams of the box strip at the midpoints of opposite sides, then mark all the corners of the cushion on the wrong side of the fabric with a pencil.

14
Cut small notches into the seam allowances on both sides of the strip at each marked corner.

15
To attach the loop box strip to one fringed seat section, lay the seat section on top of the cushion, matching notches at each corner, with the raw edge of the strip even with the finished edge of the fringe; pin in place.

16
Lift the seat section and box strip off the cushion, then machine-stitch them together along the seam line, pivoting around corners and removing pins as you work.

17
To finish, position and pin, then machine-stitch the second seat section to the box strip, as in Steps 15 and 16, leaving a 12-inch opening in the center of the last side for turning.

18
Clip the seam allowances to ease the fringe at the corners, ensuring a good fit.

19
Turn the cover right side out.

20
To insert the foam cushion into the cover, fold the cushion into a V and guide it through the opening in the cover; slip-stitch the opening closed.

21
Position the cushion on the stool, tying the ribbons to the stool legs.

11

Hand towels with illustration

THE EXQUISITE BEAUTY of an etched engraving can now be captured on linen. With a simple transfer process associated with the ordinary T-shirt, curling lines and undulating shapes can now embellish any piece of flat-weave fabric, including your finest linen towels.

For beautiful line art, visit vintage or antique print dealers, searching for black-and-white engravings of cherubs, fruit, or birds in flight. Or, if you prefer to coordinate your bathroom furnishings, like your wallpaper, to your hand towels, use a section of leftover paper, harvesting a favorite motif. Then transfer the art to a face towel or even a shower curtain, using this simple technique. The joy of living with art will be underscored and further enhance your spa treatments.

materials

2 white or cream linen towels with flat weave

Black-and-white line art, or as desired (Featured: George Brickman, *The Universal Penman*, New York: Dover Publications, 1998)

2 sheets photo transfer paper

Teflon cookie sheet (or plain cookie sheet lined with double layer a unbleached muslin)

You will also need: access to laser color copier; scissors; masking tape; iron; scrap paper

directions

Note: This process works as well with full-color art. Follow the directions to create an iron-on transfer for any project of your choice.

1
To prepare photo transfer art, go to a local copy store that has a laser color copier, bringing your chosen artwork and hand towels with you.

2
First, use a black-and-white copier to size and copy the artwork onto plain white paper, enlarging or reducing until satisfied.

3
Print a mirror image of the artwork on transfer paper, using a laser color copier; repeat for the second motif.

4 To prepare a transfer image for application to the towels, carefully trim around the perimeter of the image, getting as close as possible without cutting into art.

5 Lay a hand towel face up on the cookie sheet.

6 Empty an iron of any water and preheat it to hot (linen setting), making certain the steam feature is turned off.

7 Press the hand towel with the hot iron, and while the towel is still hot, position a transfer facedown on the center bottom of the towel, or as desired.
Note: If the towel has sewn borders, keep the image ¼ inch away from any border to avoid an uneven surface, which will cause uneven printing.

8 Press the transfer image lightly with the iron for 20 to 30 seconds to set up adhesion.

9 Continue pressing the transfer, using even pressure for 1 to 2 minutes, moving the iron in a circular motion and pressing down all sections of the transfer paper.

13

10 To reveal the image on the towel, peel up one corner of the transfer paper, then the rest, until all the paper is removed from the towel.
Note: If the paper does not come off, cover the exposed image with scrap paper to protect the image and reheat the stuck section with the hot iron, removing the scrap paper and peeling up the remaining transfer paper.

11 Repeat Steps 6 through 11 to transfer art to the opposite end of the towel, and to the second towel.

Silver and gold-leaf candles

IT HAS BEEN SAID that it is in the shadows that we distinguish what we see. Such is the mystery and nature of candlelight. Glimmering in a dark room, a lighted candle seems to animate objects. It moves them to liquid form as the flame flickers. Candlelight has a way of softening forms and quieting our internal moods, causing us to lose our edges, too. And because this tranquilizing effect is almost universal, we seek out candles of every shape and size.

If you are going to use candles in your sanctuary, especially around the tub, choose fat and short candles with a low center of gravity for safety. Place them far from anything flammable, and do not leave them unattended when lit.

If you choose to decorate your candles, you might try laying on a little extra shimmer by way of metal leaf. Since it requires no adhesive, only static electricity, you can apply bits of silver or gold leaf in minutes and provide an extra glow to your experience.

15

materials

Pillar candles, 3 in. diameter × 6 in. high

Book of metal leaf: aluminum leaf (or silver leaf or composition gold leaf)

You will also need: pencil; cotton ball

directions

Note: Work in a draft-free space.

1

Peel cellophane wrap from a candle and lay on its side on a flat work surface.

2

Open the book of metal leaf, and use a finger to tear away a piece approximately 2 inches wide from one sheet.

3

Carrying the leaf on your finger, position and press your finger on the side of the candle, tapping the leaf in place with the end of a pencil.

4

Continue tearing, carrying, and pressing leaf onto the surface of the candle until it is decorated as desired.
Note: The leaf will appear in a broken pattern on the candle.

5

To burnish the leaf, carefully rub it with a cotton ball, smoothing the leaf and adhering it to the candle wax.
Note: Some flaking will occur.

Silver-leaf box

A SMALL SILVER BOX may be just the memento you can make to keep something with special meaning, perhaps a lock of hair, a handwritten note from a child, or several foreign coins saved from a vacation. When you have finished your box, you can stand it in your altar or give it to a friend, enclosing something of symbolic value.

materials

Round wooden box with lift-off lid, approximately 3½ in. diameter

Acrylic white paint

Clear acrylic sealer

Quick-dry synthetic gold size

10 to 12 sheets aluminum leaf

Acrylic gold paint

You will also need: fine-grit sandpaper; soft cloth; rubber gloves; paintbrush; four pencils; cotton balls; scrap white paper

directions

Caution: Work in a well-ventilated space.

1
Sand the box lid, edges, and rims, making certain the surfaces are satiny smooth; use a soft, damp cloth to remove the dust.

2
Repeat Step 1 for the box bottom.

3
Prime all the surfaces of the box lid and bottom using white paint; let the box dry overnight, then repeat Steps 1 and 2.

4
Apply a thin coat of sealer; let the box dry overnight, then repeat.

5
Following the manufacturer's directions and wearing rubber gloves, apply a thin coat of size to the exterior sections of the box lid.

6
Set the lid right side up on two pencils spaced so that rim is elevated off the work surface.

7
Repeat Step 5 to apply a coat of size to the exterior of the box bottom, then invert the box and set it on two pencils spaced apart.

8
Allow the size on the lid and bottom to dry to tack, about 10 minutes.
Note: A finger touched lightly on the surface will make a tick *sound.*

9
To cut squares of leaf, open the book, hold four sheets of leaf (and their protective tissue), and freehand cut squares, each approximately ¾ inch; repeat for twelve more sheets.
Note: Do not worry if the squares are not perfect; when the leaf is burnished, the spaces between uneven squares will be faint or blend together.

10
When the size is tacky, transfer the pieces of leaf to the sized areas on the box and lid using your fingertip as follows: Touch one square with your fingertip to lift, carry, and position it on the sized surface; use the eraser end of a pencil to tamp the leaf in place.
Note: The leaf cannot be repositioned without tearing.

11
Repeat Step 10 until the exteriors of the box lid and bottom are covered with leaf, cutting more squares of leaf as necessary.

12
Allow the box and lid to dry overnight.

13
When dry, use a cotton ball to burnish all the leafed areas, brushing away loose flakes with a dry paintbrush.

14
Apply two coats of gold paint to the interiors of the box lid and bottom, allowing the paint to dry between coats; let dry 2 hours.

15
To protect the leafed finish, apply two coats of sealer, allowing the first coat to dry before applying the second.

17

Silver-leaf frames

NOTHING HIGHLIGHTS a photograph more than the quiet gleam of a silver frame. Here a group of silver frames hold photographs as well as scripted sayings. The appeal of this grouping is that each frame was transformed from a plain wooden frame to the sparkling frames you see here.

With just a few materials, essentially metal leaf and varnish, you can apply a beautiful silver (or gold) patina to any flat-sided frame. Because they are so reasonably priced, you will not worry about surrounding your bath with these framed pictures and mementos bordered in precious-looking metal.

materials

Varnished picture frame with wide, flat sides

Quick-dry synthetic gold size

Book of aluminum leaf (or silver leaf)

Clear acrylic sealer

You will also need: rubber gloves; paintbrush; four pencils; cotton balls; soft cloth

directions

Note: Work in a well-ventilated, draft-free space.

1
Dismantle the frame, backing, and glass, setting the frame on a protected work surface.

2
Following the manufacturer's directions and wearing rubber gloves, apply a thin coat of size to all sections of frame front.

3
Set the frame right side up on four pencils, spaced so that the frame is elevated off the work surface, and allow the size to reach tack, about 10 minutes.
Note: A finger touched lightly on the surface will make a tick sound.

4
Meanwhile, prepare the aluminum leaf. Open the book, hold four sheets of leaf (and their protective tissue), and freehand cut squares, each approximately ¾ inch; repeat for twelve more sheets.
Note: Do not worry if the squares are not perfect; when the leaf is burnished, the spaces between uneven squares will be faint or blend together.

5
When the size is tacky, transfer the pieces of leaf to the sized areas on the frame using your fingertip as follows: Touch one square with your fingertip to lift, carry, and position it on the edge of the frame; use the eraser end of a pencil to tamp the leaf in place.
Note: The leaf cannot be repositioned without tearing.

6
Repeat Steps 4 and 5 until the frame is covered with leaf, cutting more squares of leaf as necessary.

7
Allow the frame to dry overnight.

8
To leaf the back and edges of the frame, turn the frame over and follow Steps 2 through 7.

9
Use a clean paintbrush to remove loose flakes of leaf, then buff the surfaces gently with a cotton ball.

10
To protect the leafed finish, apply two coats of sealer, allowing the first coat to dry before applying the second.

19

Faucet sachets

IN AN ENTIRELY convenient yet beautiful way, you can infuse your bathwater with inspiring fragrance using these delicate sachets. Deceivingly sturdy, each embroidered sachet is filled with a rich floral potpourri made from chamomile flowers, rose petals, and lavender buds. However, the variety of herbal ingredients available is wide, and you can select a combination that suits what your body and spirit need. Once you have made and filled your sachets, hang them over the faucet in your bathtub, allowing the herbal essences to provide their aromatic gifts.

20

materials

YIELD: 2 SACHETS WITH RIBBON TIE

Two 11½ × 5–in. rectangles of embroidered and crinkled organza in light green or like fabric

Matching thread

1 yd. satin ribbon, ¼ in. wide

Potpourri (see page 32)

Optional

BEAD DETAIL FOR TWO SACHETS:

8 leaf-shaped glass beads in light green, each ¾ in. long

32 glass seed beads in garnet

Four 5-mm round glass beads in garnet

Beading needle and thread

You will also need: iron; sewing machine with zigzag capability; straight pins; safety pin; scissors

directions

1
Lay one organza rectangle vertically on a protected work surface, wrong side up.

2
Fold and press a scant ¼-inch hem along each long side, then machine-stitch, using zigzag, to conceal the raw edge.

3
Lay the rectangle vertically on the work surface, wrong side up.

4
To make the top ribbon casing, double-fold the top edge down ¼ inch, then ⅜ inch, pressing to secure.

5
Topstitch a hem ⅛ inch from the edge of the fold to complete the casing.

6
To make the bottom casing, repeat Step 5 at the bottom edge.

7 Fold the rectangle in half widthwise, edges even, right sides facing, using pins to secure sides.

8 To make the pouch, machine-stitch the sides ⅛ inch from the edges, beginning at the bottom edge and stopping at the seam for the ribbon casing.

9 Turn the pouch right side out.

10 To make the second pouch, repeat Steps 1 through 9.

11 To connect the pouches, tie a knot at one end of the length of ribbon, attaching a safety pin at the opposite end.

12 Insert the safety pin into the ribbon casing of one pouch, threading the ribbon through the entire casing, pushing the pin out through the entry hole, and removing the safety pin. Do not cut the ribbon.

13 Repeat Step 12 with the second pouch.

14 Remove the safety pin, and tie that ribbon end in a knot.

15 Optional: To make beaded leaf drops at the bottom corners of the sachets:

a. Insert the beading needle with 8 inches of thread from the inside corner, ending on the right side of the pouch.

b. String onto the needle 1 leaf and 4 seed beads, sliding the beads down the thread to the fabric.

c. Reinsert the needle through the leaf, skipping over the seed beads and anchoring the thread to the corner fabric by taking several small stitches.

d. String on 1 garnet bead and 2 seed beads.

e. Reinsert the needle through the garnet bead, anchoring the thread to the corner fabric near the top of the leaf.

f. Insert the needle through the second leaf and 4 seed beads.

g. Reinsert the needle through the leaf, anchoring the thread to the corner fabric as in Step e.

h. Repeat Steps a through g for the remaining three corners of the pouches.

16 Fill each pouch half full of potpourri. (See herbal paper sachet potpourri recipe on page 32.)

17 Gather the casing of one sachet tightly on the ribbon, tying it with a knot to secure.

18 Gather the casing of the second sachet tightly on the ribbon at the opposite end, tying the end of the ribbon with a knot to secure.

19 To use the sachets, wrap the ribbon once around the tub faucet, positioning one sachet under the running water and the second in the bathwater.

21

The altar

CREATING A SACRED PLACE in your home is another way to care for and honor yourself. One way to achieve this is by setting up a little altar. Whether they are simple shelves or windowsills, or a single piece of furniture dedicated to this purpose, altars are living testimonies to what is important to us. By gathering and arranging symbolic objects that represent the significant people, places, and experiences in our lives in one holy place, we are pooling the energy of the thoughts and feelings that form the core of who we are.

The featured altar is a plain cabinet with a front glass panel painted in a vine and floral motif. This painting technique was borrowed from a favorite folk art tradition of reverse painting on glass, in which images are painted on one side of the glass and viewed from the other. Shelves hold mementos and special objects. If you prefer another design, be aware that you can easily be guided by placing a design behind the glass and tracing it free-hand with a paintbrush. Or you can decoupage images on the glass, choosing especially meaningful motifs and illustrations. The altar is your living testimony, so feel free to decorate and fill it with whatever you desire. And don't forget to add new objects, or to change the ones that are there, as the spirit moves you.

23

materials

Wooden cabinet with door with glass panel (Featured panel measures 7⅞ × 12⅞ in.)

Glass or china paint:

For Pattern 1, Vines and Leaves:
  Burnt sienna

For Pattern 2, Vines, Flowers, and Leaves:
  For leaves without tone: Light green
  For leaves with tone: Dark green
  For vines: Light green
  For flowers: Salmon and white

Paintbrushes:

No. 2 liner brush
No. 10/0 liner brush

You will also need: screwdriver; glass cleaner; paper towels; access to photocopier; 2 patterns (see pages 108-109); newspaper; freezer paper

The altar

directions

Note: Patterns can be adapted, reduced or enlarged, or used in portions.

1 Use a screwdriver to remove the screws, then the glass, from the door of the cabinet; set the screws aside.

2 Remove spots from all surfaces of the glass using spray cleaner and paper towels.

3 Copy each pattern, enlarging it by ascending percentages; or copy and test-fit your patterns until they fit the glass panel.

4 To prepare a palette for the paint, lay a sheet of freezer paper on a flat surface, dropping small blobs of color 3 inches apart.

5 On a separate piece of paper, practice the long comma stroke for vines: use a No. 2 liner brush dipped in paint; press the bristles of the brush lightly, then firmly, against the paper, drawing a gentle curve, and lifting the bristles up to end in a point in one smooth motion.

6 To practice the short comma stroke for leaves, use a No. 2 liner brush dipped in paint; press the bristles lightly against the paper, then firmly in the middle, lifting gently as the stroke is completed; for plumper leaves, use two overlapping strokes.

7 To practice the blunt comma stroke for single petals, use a No. 2 liner brush; press the bristles firmly against the paper, lifting up gradually to end the stroke in a sharp point at the inside of the petal, near the stamen.

8 For all stamens, dots, and accent strokes, load a No. 10/0 liner brush with paint.

9 Tilt the brush handle toward you, touch the tip of the brush to the paper, then lift to produce a tiny, round dot or C-shaped stroke.

10 To paint the glass, lay Pattern 1 on a protected work surface, and lay the glass over the pattern, aligning the edges of the glass and the marked rectangle on the pattern.

11 Use a No. 2 liner brush to trace all the vines and leaves indicated on the pattern in burnt sienna; let the paint dry.

12 Lay the glass panel, painted side up, on Pattern 2, aligning the edges of the glass and the marked rectangle on the pattern.
a. Use a No. 2 liner brush to trace all the vines, plain leaves, and stems indicated on the pattern in light green.
b. Use a No. 2 liner brush to paint all secondary leaves indicated in dark green.
c. Use a No. 2 liner brush to paint all flowers salmon; let dry, then go back to each petal, accenting the end, using a No. 10/0 brush and white paint; paint the stamen dots using a No. 10/0 brush and brown paint.

13 Assess your work, adding strokes to indicate more detail as desired.

14 Let the paint cure overnight.

15 Reinstall the painted glass in the cabinet, painted side in.

24

Candlesticks with chandelier crystal accents

THERE IS LITTLE to compare to the beauty of cut glass, especially when it reflects light like cut crystal. For a touch of sparkle, you can collect mismatched chandelier crystals and decorate a candlestick in a few minutes. The candlestick should be sturdy, having a heavy base to counterbalance the crystals that are hooked around the rim of the candle cup. Visit antique and lighting-repair shops to find old chandelier crystals, then accent a pair of candlesticks.

materials

5 or 6 chandelier crystals with wire hooks, as desired

Metal candlestick with rimmed candle cup

Optional

medium-gauge aluminum wire

ruler

junky scissors

pliers

directions

1
Optional: to wire a chandelier crystal without a hanging hook, measure and cut a 1-inch length of wire, using ruler and scissors.

25

2
To make a hanging hook, use pliers to bend the cut wire into an "S" shape.

3
Insert one end of the hook into the hole in crystal.

4
Balance the hook on the opposite end of the rim of the candle cup.

5
Repeat Step 4, distributing crystals evenly around the rim.

bathing and body
care rituals

Be alert to those brief moments during the day

when you experience

your fundamental self

behind a breath, a feeling,

a sensation.

—Deepak Chopra

IF WE ARE TO REALLY RELAX, if we are to truly reconnect to ourselves and find out who we are and what we value, we first have to hear and follow the yearnings of our heart that are communicated through our senses. And nowhere are our senses felt more strongly than in the rituals of bathing. In the simple act of immersing our bodies in water, or in scrubbing our skin until it tingles, we connect to our fundamental beingness and receive its most intimate messages.

Simply put, bathing is more than hygiene; it is sensational. The bath is a womb for the soul. Fundamental serenity can be achieved in the quiet ceremony of being immersed in water, warm and flowing, moving over the mounds of our flesh, fitting its contours, and resonating with our internal aqueous systems. It is the water content already in our bodies, perhaps, that allows bathing to restore our primal connections to ourselves. In any case, it is enough to know that the sheer pleasure of this rite is all we need to feel to establish self-care rituals as a routine in our lives.

But for these rituals to truly relax and restore the body, mind, and spirit, we need to be willing to release the attachments we have to the outside world, however compelling they may seem. We need to give in to the possibilities that await us in this steamy oasis, if only briefly. When we do the world will slip away, and we will stand on our own inner

shores, filled with our deepest desires, our thoughts, our loves, and our needs, all ebbing and flowing in such an immense and profound quiet that we might feel like we are merging with the oceanic force of the universe.

This powerful communion is a gift you can give yourself. It is vital. It is deserved. These benefits are as near as your decision to retreat to your personal sanctuary, gathering up a few basics. Be ready to receive them. To do so, you need to set some time aside. Make it a daily or weekly routine. Mark your sanctuary time on your calendar. Your routines can be as simple or complex as you desire, taking only a few minutes or an hour. They can be calming or invigorating or both, depending on what you need in the moment.

If possible, select natural products with which to take care of yourself—a salt scrub or loofah to exfoliate, a milk bath to moisturize, a creamy soap to clean, an herbal solution to rinse, a drop of fragrant oil to inspire. With little more than the ingredients you have on your kitchen shelves, you can make the most soothing and luxuriant concoctions. You will find that in their simple ministrations you will further restore contact with yourself.

Begin your rituals by lighting scented candles and when you do, you will almost immediately begin to relinquish your hold on the outside world. The quiet light and soft aromas will transport you away from your daily concerns, drawing you into your immediate surroundings, your personal sanctuary.

Simultaneously, you will notice that your senses will seem to come more alive in the tranquility of this personal space. So much so that you may be able to distinguish for the first time the difference between the fragrance of lavender and eucalyptus, as each herb is emitted from the little sachets you have slipped into the pockets of your shower curtain. Or, you may feel sudden pleasure in the listening to the strains of a measure of music; never have they sounded so soaring and clear. And when you rest your head on the pretty tub pillow you have placed within the curve of a rose garland, you will feel tension leaving your body as you surrender to this ethereal world you have created in your own home.

While you have surely planned a regimen to pamper and heal your body and mind using the special preparations you have made yourself, do not rush immediately into any vigorous procedures. Instead, spend a little time just being, just floating, just feeling. Submerge your body beneath the water and pay closer attention to your self, and to the meaning of just being you on the planet, right now, right here where you may come to know the very special purpose for which you have come, a purpose only you can fulfill.

Be prepared and expectant. Allow yourself to merge with your surroundings. Untold gifts await you.

29

Patch-pocket shower curtain with herbs

IF YOU WANT YOUR BATH to be more of a retreat, be sure to add herbal fragrances, especially fresh foliage, that help you relax. A translucent shower curtain can be the perfect place to start. When drawn, it will keep the steam contained in the area of the bathtub. And if you add patch pockets to your shower curtain, you can fill them with aromatic sachets or fresh herbal sprigs. Gather a few branches of eucalyptus or rosemary, breaking off small sprigs, and place them in the pockets of the shower curtain. Or make tea bag–style sachets, slipping three or four into pockets scattered over the curtain. The steam and moisture will activate the plants' fragrances, filling your space with divine scent. Be aware that the sachets are more concentrated in scent, so you will need fewer of them to fill your room with fragrance.

materials

YIELD: 25 POCKETS

Shower curtain in sheer organdy

For patch pockets:

1 yd. sheer organdy

Matching thread

Herbs:

25 fresh herbal sprigs (i.e., eucalyptus, rosemary, thyme, or rose petals)

Optional

10 herbal paper sachets (see page 32)

You will also need: iron; straight pins; sewing machine

directions

1 To prepare patch pockets for the shower curtain, measure and cut twenty-five 5-inch squares from the organdy.

2 Double-fold a ¼-inch hem on each side of each square, pressing in place using an iron set to the fabric type.

3 Randomly position and pin the pockets across the curtain or as desired.

4 Topstitch each pocket to the curtain along three sides a scant ¼ inch from the edges, leaving the top open.

31

5 Hang the shower curtain, filling several pockets with herbal sachets, or all pockets with fresh herbal sprigs, as desired.

Herbal paper sachets

THERE ARE SO MANY flowers and herbs you can combine to fill these little tea bag–style sachets, you may have trouble deciding which ones to use. One solution is to make several batches of potpourris, filling the sachets until all the ingredients are used up. Then store them in a jar or wrap them in a pretty container and present them to friends.

These sachets can be used directly in the bathwater, or they can be secreted between the layers of folded linen. They can also be slipped into the pockets of the patch-pocket shower curtain featured on page 30. However you decide to use them, remember first to provide for your needs, choosing aromatherapeutic ingredients that help you. If you need to relax, choose jasmine, rose, or lavender; to invigorate your spirit and increase your circulation, choose eucalyptus or peppermint; to inspire sensuality, choose ylang-ylang, rose, or sandalwood.

For more information on the aromatherapeutic properties of other herbs and flowers, see pages 106–107.

32

materials

YIELD: 10 SACHETS

1 sheet silk paper

Cotton thread

Potpourri:

20 tbsp. lavender buds (or dried rose petals, balsam needles, citrus peels, chamomile flowers or as desired)

½ cup oak moss

Essential oil to match chosen dried potpourri

You will also need: pinking shears or scissors; measuring spoons; large, clean jar, like a mayonnaise jar, with screw-on lid; sewing machine with zigzag capability

directions

Note: Prepare the potpourri one day ahead as follows: Tear the moss into ½-inch pieces and place it in the jar, along with 20 tablespoons of your chosen dried material; add 10 drops of matching fragrance oil and stir; close the lid tightly and store in a dark place overnight.

1 Cut ten rectangles from the silk paper, each measuring 3 × 6 inches.

2 Fold a paper rectangle in half widthwise; repeat for the remaining rectangles.

3 Use a sewing machine set to zigzag stitch to topstitch three sides of a pouch, ¼ inch from the edge, leaving the top open; repeat for the remaining rectangles.

33

4 Fill the cavity of each pouch half full with 2 tablespoons of potpourri.

5 Topstitch across the top of the sachet, ¼ inch from the top edge; repeat for the remaining sachets.

6 Store the sachets in the jar with the lid screwed on loosely.

Colored and scented candles

To set the mood in your bathroom sanctuary, you will most assuredly want to include candlelight. While the glow of a candle flame is notably flattering to most skin, the candle can also infuse the air with aromatic essences that confer healthful benefits. The menthol in mint, for example, can invigorate you. Rosemary can improve your memory, or so it is said. When the herb is near the heat of the flame, it emits the fragrance you have added.

To make your own scented candles, add a few drops of essential oil to melted wax and roll your candle in it. While you are adding scent, you can add the color of your choice. All you need are a few pieces of crayon. The crayon is added to melted paraffin, and the candle is rolled in the paraffin, coating the outside with both fragrance and color.

Be especially careful when working with melted wax. It is extremely flammable and should never be unattended. See the important cautions listed with the directions.

34

materials

3 to 4 blocks or 1 lb. household
  paraffin wax

Cream or white dripless paraffin pillar
  candle or candles, 3 to 6 in. high

Wax crayon in color desired

Liquid candle scent or essential oil,
  as desired

You will also need: aluminum foil;
2 flat-bottomed pans—one large
stainless steel roasting pan with rack,
and one smaller disposable aluminum
foil roasting pan; candy thermometer;
stainless steel measuring spoons; rubber
gloves; 2 spiked corncob holders; junky
tablespoon; nylon stocking

directions

Caution: Wax is flammable and must never be melted over an open flame. Use a thermometer to maintain a temperature of 180° Fahrenheit or below.

1 Tear off several feet of aluminum foil from its roll and lay it on a flat work surface.

2 Set the large roasting pan with rack on two burners of a stove and pour in water until it covers the rack.

3 Set the smaller foil pan on the rack, and place in it three blocks of paraffin.

4 Heat the water to a boil, then simmer, allowing the water to keep the wax liquid. *Caution: Use a thermometer to keep the wax temperature below 180° Fahrenheit.*

5 Peel the crayon and break or cut it into six to eight pieces.

6 To color the paraffin, drop one small piece of crayon into the melted wax, stirring with spoon to blend. *Note: To intensify the color, add more crayon pieces, one at a time, until the color is as desired. To lessen the color, add more paraffin.*

7 Add 1 tablespoon of the desired fragrance, stirring quickly and carefully to blend.

8 Pull on rubber gloves and push the corncob holders into opposite ends of the candle, carefully heating the corncob holder prongs over the stove for easy insertion if necessary.

9 Hold the candle at opposite ends using the corncob holders; lower it into the paraffin rolling and skimming it to coat the exterior. *Caution: Do not rest the candle on the bottom of the pan; doing so can melt a flat section in the candle.*

10 Lift the candle out of the paraffin and stand it upright for 20 to 25 seconds. *Note: Some drips on the candle surface are unavoidable and are a natural and attractive part of the hand-rolling process.*

11 Repeat Steps 9 and 10 until the intensity of color is as desired.

12 Remove the corncob holders, then conceal their holes with a careful dip in the melted paraffin.

13 Stand the candle upright on the aluminum foil; wait 10 minutes.

14 Continue coating candles, using different scents and colors if desired.

15 To remove any drips or unevenness at the bottoms of the candles, stand them in the heated pan to melt the bottoms flat.

16 To finish, buff the sides of the candles, using a wadded-up stocking.

35

Bath linen ensemble

ACCENTING IS ONE of the easiest ways to perk up flat- and piqué-weave bath linen. Known for their absorbency and snowy white color, piqué towels look even bolder and crisper with border ribbons. All you need to do to create a bright bathroom ensemble is collect your towels, washcloths, and bath mat, a few yards of ribbon, and your sewing machine.

The best ribbon for this project is grosgrain. It is sturdy and colorfast, and its edges are woven, making for a neat finish. The ribbon also comes in a wide choice of widths, colors, and patterns. Whether with zippy narrow stripes or polka dots, plaid or plain, ribbon can add life to tired linens in an instant and inspire you to wrap yourself up with the thought that you may not want to put on clothes for a very long time.

materials

Cotton waffle piqué bath towel, hand towel, washcloth, and bath mat

Grosgrain ribbon*

5⅓ yd. blue-and-white-striped grosgrain ribbon, 1¼ in. wide:

For bath towel, 26 in. wide: approximately 54 in.

For hand towel, 18 in. wide: approximately 38 in.

For washcloth, 12 in. square: approximately 26 in.

For bath mat, 28 × 22 in.: approximately 92 in.

Matching thread

You will also need: ruler; scissors; straight pins; sewing machine.

directions

4 To sew the hand towel, repeat Step 3, positioning the ribbons 2½ inches above the bottom edge.

1 Measure and cut the ribbon as follows: for the bath towel, two lengths, each equal to the width plus 1 inch for side hems; for the hand towel, two lengths, each equal to the width plus 1 inch for side hems; for the washcloth, two lengths, each equal to the width plus 1 inch for the side hems; for the bath mat, four lengths, two equal to the length of the mat minus 4 inches and two equal to the width of the mat minus 4 inches.

5 To sew the bath towel, repeat Step 3, positioning the ribbons 4 inches above the bottom edge.

6 To sew the bath mat, lay the mat lengthwise on a flat work surface; fold and press ½-inch hems at the ends of the ribbon lengths. Position the ribbons in a rectangle, approximately 4 inches from all sides of the bath mat.
Note: Position the shorter lengths across the width and the longer lengths across the length, tucking the folded ends under at the corners. Pin and machine-stitch the ribbons in place a scant ⅛ inch from the ribbons' edges.

2 To prepare the ribbons for all but the bath mat, fold and press ½-inch side hems at each end of each length of ribbon.

3 To sew the washcloth, center the ribbon across the width of the cloth, 1½ inches above the bottom edge, pinning and machine-stitching the ribbon in place a scant ⅛ inch from the ribbon's edges. Repeat to secure the ribbon to the opposite side of the cloth.

37

Hand towels with fringe

AS DAINTILY AND beautifully decorated as some hand towels can be, we tend to shy away from using them. Their fabric may be too delicate, and their usually diminutive size discourages us. So they are left out for their decorative value only, some so elaborately embroidered or embellished that they must be considered art.

While this is a lovely and often necessary indulgence for our spirits, we usually need our linen to work harder. An attractive and practical alternative to standard-size hand towels is to make ones that are oversize using any sturdy even-weave cotton you like. (Cotton is absorbent and easy to care for.) Fabrics that have true weaves can be frayed to create a pretty fringe. Choose a plaid so that the threads can guide your cutting, fraying, and sewing.

materials

1 yd. sturdy, even-weave cotton fabric in plaid, 36 in. wide

Matching thread

You will also need: scissors; sewing machine with zigzag capability

directions

Note: Warp threads run top to bottom; weft threads run at a right angle to the warp threads to create the widthwise grain.

1 Lay the fabric lengthwise on a flat work surface.

2 Cut the fabric in half lengthwise to create two pieces, each measuring 18 inches wide and 36 inches long.

3 To make side hems, double-fold a ⅜-inch hem along each long side, pinning and top-stitching ⅛ inch from the edge of the fold.

4 To begin the fringe, with very sharp scissors cut the top and bottom edges straight and even, using the weft thread to guide your cutting.

5 To fray the top and bottom edges, carefully use a pin to pick out individual weft threads, pulling each thread free from the fabric; discard the loose threads.

6 Continue picking and pulling out weft threads until the fringes measure 2½ inches or as long as you desire.

7 Machine-stitch across the fabric where the fringes meet woven fabric, using a zigzag stitch.

Circular seat cushion

RECYCLING A less-than-perfect metal chair is a wise decision if the chair is structurally sound. Thereafter, you can transform its appearance by changing one simple detail, the seat cover. With only fabric and a staple gun you can beautify the most ordinary find. And you will love making space for this little necessity.

materials

Chair with set-in seat cushion

Sturdy striped cotton fabric (or other fabric, as desired)

Optional

polyester batting, 1-in. loft

You will also need: pencil; scissors; staple gun and staples

directions

1 Remove the seat cushion from the chair frame.

2 Remove the old fabric and padding from the cushion, reserving the seat support. *Note: The support may be made of wood, heavy particleboard, or chipboard.*

3 Use the seat support as a template to cut out the new seat covering and padding as follows:

a. Spread the fabric wrong side up and lay the seat support on it.

b. Trace around the perimeter of the seat support; make another outline, adding enough for the depth of the cushion plus 6 inches. Cut along the outside penciled line.

c. Lay the seat support on the batting, trimming the batting even with the perimeter of the seat support.

4 To attach the new cover to the seat support, lay the fabric wrong side up, centering the batting in the marked circle.

5 Center the seat support on top of the batting and fabric.

6 Pull the opposite edges of the fabric along the lengthwise grain, bringing the fabric around to the top of the seat support and stapling it in place 1½ inches from the edge of the seat.

7 Repeat Step 6 on the crosswise grain, then continue working opposite sides to keep the cover smooth until the fabric is completely secured to the seat support.

8 Reinstall the newly covered cushion in the chair frame.

Scented milk bath

IF YOU WANT TO FEEL like a queen, this luxurious milk bath is the answer. It will pamper and soothe your skin, whether it is dry or irritated. The fat in the milk is moisturizing and nourishing, as is the honey. After you prepare the mixture, pour it into warm bathwater, swooshing the water to blend. Soak your body for at least 20 minutes and feel the difference.

ingredients

YIELD: FOR IMMEDIATE USE
ENOUGH FOR ONE BATH

1 qt. whole milk

¼ cup honey

20 drops rose essential oil*, or as desired

*Caution: *Before using an essential oil, be sure to follow the health cautions contained on the copyright page iv.*

You will also need: stainless steel measuring cups; glass eyedropper; large glass bowl; stainless steel spoon

Do not use any equipment with copper, aluminum, cast-iron or Teflon finishes.

41

directions

1
Measure, pour, and stir milk, honey, and rose oil in glass bowl.

2
Pour into tub full of warm water, swooshing to blend.

Hand towels with lace

WHETHER THEY ARE laid out for show or for serious use, you can count on these towels to serve you well because they are made from absorbent cotton. Although you may be reluctant to put even a crease in something so pristine, you will love the indulgence of drying your face with these elegant but hardworking towels.

It is so easy to transform ordinary towels using only a few lengths of lace. For well-deserved pampering, make several lace-edged towels, using different lace styles, and keep them in a neat stack on your sink. This way they will be nearby when you wash your face, ready both to dry your skin and to meet your needs for visual beauty in your surroundings.

materials

2 cotton hand towels

Cotton lace* (approximately 1 yd., 1½ in. wide)

Matching thread

You will also need: straight pins; scissors; sewing machine with zigzag capability

directions

1
Lay a towel lengthwise and right side up on a flat work surface.

2
To calculate how much lace you will need for each towel, measure the width of the towel and add ¾ inch; then multiply the measurement by the number of edges you wish to decorate.

3
To prepare lace for two towel edges, cut two lengths of lace, each equal to the width of the towel plus ¾ inch.

4
Fold and press a ⅜-inch hem at each end of a length of lace, pinning and topstitching in place using a sewing machine set to zigzag stitch.

5
Center one length of lace across the towel, laying the top edge of the lace approximately ⅜ inch above the bottom edge of the towel, using straight pins to secure.

6
Machine-stitch across the top edge of the lace a scant ⅛ inch from the edge, making certain to keep the lace flat.

7
To stabilize the lace, machine-stitch across it, ¼ inch below the first line of stitching.

8
Repeat Steps 1 through 7 for the second towel.

Scented bath oil

NOT ONLY CAN a hot bath be soothing and cleansing but, with the right oils and fragrances, it can change your state of mind, inspiring happiness, sensuality, and healing. When you prepare your own oil and fragrance blends, you can personalize your bathing ritual, selecting a particular oil according to your need. Making your own scented bath oil is easy. All you need to do is prepare the base or carrier oil, which is often composed of several unscented oils. This combination becomes the foundation to which you add a fragrance, or essential oil, of your choice. The oils in the basic recipe can be found right in your kitchen cabinet, or at your health food store.

44

materials

YIELD: ENOUGH FOR 12 BATHS

For Unscented Base Oil:
5 oz. sweet almond oil

2½ oz. olive oil

2 oz. canola oil

1 oz. apricot kernel oil

1 oz. sesame oil

½ oz. wheat germ oil

Oil and Fragrance Blends

For Invigorating Citrus Blend:
Base oil recipe

Essential oils*:
½ tsp. mandarin orange

½ tsp. grapefruit

½ tsp. lemon

For Relaxing Lavender Blend:
Base oil recipe

Essential oils*:
1 tsp. lavender

½ tsp. bergamot

¼ tsp. cedar

For Warming Vanilla Blend:
Base oil recipe

Essential oils:
½ tsp. vanilla

½ tsp. sandalwood

You will also need: large glass measuring cup; stainless steel measuring spoons; glass container with cap to store; rubbing alcohol

Do not use any equipment with copper, aluminum, cast-iron or Teflon finishes.

*Caution: *Before using an essential oil, be sure to follow the health cautions contained on the copyright page iv.*

directions

After you make up your preparation, store it in a cool, dark place to preserve it longer. When you are ready for a heavenly bathing experience, add 1 ounce to your bathwater, stir to blend, then slide into the tub and enjoy the effects. Or, if you prefer, you can use this recipe directly on your skin as a moisturizer or for massage. Be aware that citrus oils and bergamot can cause photosensitivity. Do not expose skin to sun after use.

1
To make unscented base oil, combine ingredients in glass measuring cup.

2
For fragrances, use measuring spoons to add selected oils. Clean oils off of spoons with rubbing alcohol.

3
Transfer oil mixture to glass container, securing cap.

4
Shake container to blend oils, then store in a cool, dark place.

5
To use: Add 1 ounce to your bathwater. Or you can use the mixture directly on your skin as a moisturizer or for a massage. Please note that essential oils are highly concentrated and should not be applied directly to your skin.

45

Tub pillow

IF YOU HAVE NEVER tried a tub pillow while relaxing in the bath, you have been missing a most self-indulgent necessity. Surprisingly enough, a small foam pillow can make the difference between an impatient soak with a strained neck and a sensual submersion in endless time. While you can certainly use the bath pillow au naturel, it is well worth the time to beautify the vinyl version.

With just a few rectangles of crinkled organdy, you can make an elegant pillowcase with buttonholes through which to slip the suction cups in back. The value of using a sheer or near-sheer fabric is that it looks beautiful and crisp whether wet or dry. And, most important, this type of fabric dries quickly, helping to avoid the nasty mold that can develop easily when fabrics stay wet or damp too long.

To decorate the pillowcase, hand-stitch or hot-glue silk flowers to one corner. They can be made from ribbon, as those featured here, or artificial. The artificial flowers are frequently made from synthetics that easily bounce back to their original shapes, even after being wet.

47

materials

Plastic tub pillow with suction cups

Crinkled organza in moss green,*
approximately ¼ yd., 36 in. wide

Matching thread

Optional

4 ribbon roses (or 4 synthetic silk
flowers with 3-in.-long plastic stems)

For one full-blown ribbon rose:

¼ yd. wire-edged ribbon in variegated
salmon, 1⅞ in. wide

25 in. wire-edged ribbon in salmon
and moss green, 1¼ in. wide

Matching thread

2 leaves from artificial flower

You will also need: ruler; pencil; scissors; straight pins; sewing machine with buttonhole foot; hand-sewing needle

Tub pillow
directions

1 To calculate the organza needed for the pillowcase, measure and note the dimensions of the pillow as follows: height (A) plus 1 inch for seam allowances, and width (B) plus 1 inch for seam allowances.

2 Lay the organza on a flat work surface, crinkles running vertically, and use the measurements from Step 1 to cut two rectangles.

3 To prepare buttonholes for the back section, center one organza rectangle over the pillow and mark the top and bottom edges of each suction cup with a pencil.

4 Use a sewing machine to sew buttonholes.

5 To sew the pillowcase, position and pin the front and back sections together, right sides facing, all edges even.

6 Machine-stitch the two long sides and one short side, ½ inch from raw edges.

7 Clip the corners, and turn the case right side out.

To make ribbon roses:

a. To prepare the center rosebud, fold a ¼-yard length of salmon ribbon in half lengthwise, pressing the fold with your fingers.

b. Carefully push the ribbon from both ends along the wires to loosely gather until the ribbon measures 7 inches; fold under the raw edges at the ends and tack, using tiny hand-sewn stitches.

c. To build the center rosebud, roll the length of gathered ribbon around itself, allowing the center to stand slightly higher than the successive layers, and tacking the edges at the base to secure; set the bud aside.

d. To make one petal, cut a 5-inch length of ribbon and lay it on a flat work surface; press your finger at the midpoint of the top edge of the ribbon, folding down the ends so they are even at the bottom, and the top of the petal is a point.

e. Use a needle and thread to gather the ends of the petal, tacking the ends to the base of the rosebud.

f. To complete the rose, repeat Steps d and e for the remaining petals.

g. Repeat steps a through f for additional roses.

8 To attach the ribbon roses to the pillowcase, hand stitch in upper right hand corner.

9 Tack the single leaves and roses in a cluster, as desired.

10 Insert the pillow into the case slipping the buttonholes around the suction cups.

Scented bath salts

BATH SALTS ARE A wonderful way to add fragrance to bathwater, but their benefits go beyond smelling nice. Using bath salts is a great way to detoxify your skin because the minerals in the salts have a drawing effect. Bath salts can also be slightly drying, so use a good moisturizer after bathing with them. To use bath salts, add about 3 heaping tablespoons to warm bathwater when filling the tub. The aroma from the salts will be released into the water and the air while effortlessly providing healthful benefits. Enjoy!

ingredients

YIELD: ENOUGH FOR 3 BATHS

1 cup coarse sea salt
Rubbing alcohol

Optional

3 to 5 drops food color, as desired
10 drops essential oil*

*Caution: *Before using an essential oil, be sure to follow the health cautions contained on the copyright page iv.*

You will also need: medium-size glass mixing bowl; glass measuring cup; stainless steel spoon; glass eyedropper; glass storage container

Do not use any equipment with copper, aluminum, cast-iron or Teflon finishes.

directions

1
Measure and pour sea salt into mixing bowl.

2
Optional: To color salt, add 2 drops desired color, stirring with spoon to blend.
Note: For more intense color, add 1 to 2 drops more.

3
To scent salt, use eyedropper to add desired essential oil, mixing to distribute oil, cleaning dropper with rubbing alcohol when finished.

4
Store salt in glass container.

Scented salt scrub

SALT SCRUBS ARE AN excellent way to increase circulation and exfoliate your skin. As beneficial as salts are, they are known to have a drying effect, so oils have been added to create a restorative balance. Not only will the abrasive action of the salt in the scrub remove dead skin cells but it will open your pores, allowing them to breathe.

While in the shower or tub, when your skin is damp, scoop out a tablespoon or two and begin to massage the salt onto your skin. Work in a circular motion, starting at your extremities and moving toward your heart; hence, begin scrubbing your hands and arms. Next, scrub your feet and massage the salts on your legs. It is best for your circulation if you always work toward your heart. Do not forget to concentrate on particularly rough spots, like heels and elbows. Leave the scrub on your skin between 5 and 20 minutes, depending on how much moisturizing you need. Rinse off with clean, cool water.

50

ingredients

YIELD: APPROXIMATELY 15 APPLICATIONS

For Scrub:
3 cups fine sea salt
¾ cup olive oil
¾ cup sweet almond oil

Essential Oils* for Fragrance:
½ tsp. tea tree oil
½ tsp. eucalyptus oil
½ tbsp. peppermint oil
½ tbsp. rosemary oil
Rubbing alcohol

*Caution: *Before using an essential oil, be sure to follow the health cautions contained on the copyright page iv.*

You will also need: stainless steel measuring spoons; stainless steel measuring cups; large glass bowl; stainless steel spoon; for storage, glass container with lid

Do not use any equipment with copper, aluminum, cast-iron or Teflon finishes.

directions

Caution: Be sure not to apply salt scrub to any cuts or to just-shaven skin. It will cause skin irritation.

1
Measure and mix scrub ingredients in glass bowl.

2
Use measuring spoon to add olive and almond oil.

3
Blend thoroughly, using spoon.

4
Measure and add essential oils to scrub, stirring again being certain to clean spoon with alcohol when changing scents.

5
Store in tightly sealed glass container.

Bath and body gel

MANY SHOPS THAT sell bath and body products offer unscented bath gels and lotions. These ready-made products will allow you to customize your own healthful and appealing preparations.

materials

YIELD: ENOUGH FOR 3 OR 4 BATHS.
2 oz. unscented bath gel
5 to 10 drops essential oil*
Rubbing alcohol

*Caution: *Before using an essential oil, be sure to follow the health cautions contained on the copyright page iv.*

You will also need: glass eyedropper.

Do not use any equipment with copper, aluminum, cast-iron or Teflon finishes.

51

directions

1
Open prepared gel.

2
Use eyedropper to add 5 to 10 drops of chosen fragrance oil for every 2 ounces of gel. Clean eye dropper with rubbing alcohol when through.

3
To blend fragrance and gel, close jar and shake.

after bath care for
body and soul

The real voyage of discovery

consists not in seeking new landscapes,

but in having new eyes.

—Marcel Proust

RELAXED, RENEWED, and reconnected, you slowly stand up and leave the steamy pool that is your bathtub, reluctant to separate from the tranquil sensations born there. But do not worry. You can slow your reentry into the more defined world by continuing to pamper yourself. Smooth on body lotion or gently massage your skin with an oil blend. Then envelope your body in generously large towels, wrapping another towel snugly around your head for the pure and joyful physicality of it.

When you are dry, slip on a thick terry robe, or one that is lightweight but beautiful. Enjoy the peacefulness while you pay some attention to your insides, specifically your cells, nourishing them with mineral water or a fresh fruit smoothie you prepare from natural ingredients.

With refreshing drink in hand, relax on your bed or a chaise, and luxuriate in your sense of well-being. Tune in to your thoughts, recording your insights in a personal journal. Or relax with a book you have been wanting to read, getting lost in a new world.

And as you prepare to leave your personal sanctuary, focus one more time on the experience as you carry its grace forward into your day. Make a vow to fold this self consideration into your life while you are so acutely mindful of its life affirming benefits.

53

Bathrobe and slippers

THERE IS NO REASON to buy a brand-new robe if you love the one you have. A favorite robe is a familiar shelter, as well as an enrapturing finish to a relaxing bath. But you can perk it up by adding a quick accent. Sometimes a detail is all you need to raise your spirits.

Here, a bouncy pom-pom fringe was added to a cozy terry-cloth bathrobe. The pom-poms were easy to secure to the front panels, collar, and cuffs. The plaited portion of the fringe was rolled and laid in the seam, looking very much like piping. Then the roll was secured with small hand stitches, allowing the pom-poms to dangle freely.

If you prefer a more sturdy attachment, conceal the plait portion of the fringe inside the seams. Just know that this process requires you to take apart those seams of the robe you wish to decorate.

Another quick idea is to add pom-poms to a pair of slippers. Snip individual pom-poms from a fringe in a contrasting color, or buy a bag of single pom-poms and attach them using fabric glue.

54

materials

Pom-pom fringe*

For robe: approximately 3⅔ yd.*
  pom-pom fringe in contrasting color

For slippers: approximately 1 yd.
  pom-pom fringe or 30 single
  pom-poms in contrasting color

Matching thread

You will also need: tape measure;
scissors; straight pins; hand-sewing
needle; fabric glue

directions

For Slippers:

*1

To prepare pom-poms from a plaited fringe, snip off about 15 for each slipper.

2

To affix each pom-pom, apply a dab of fabric glue to one side of the pom-pom, then position and press the pom-pom in place on the slipper, glue side down.

directions

For Bathrobe:

1 To calculate the amount of fringe needed for your robe, use a tape measure to measure the length of the seam from the bottom edge of the front panel, around the neck or collar, and down to the bottom edge of the opposite front panel, adding 2 inches for tucking ends into seams; for cuffs, use a tape measure to measure the circumference of a cuff, adding 2 inches for overlapping the plait; double the measurement to include the second cuff.

2 To add the length of pom-pom fringe to your finished robe, begin at the bottom edge of one front panel as follows: Open about 1 inch of the seam, slipping the raw end of the plait into the seam; roll the plait to resemble a tube, then slip-stitch the opening closed. Position and pin the remaining length of fringe along the seams, ending at the bottom edge of the opposite front panel.

3 To secure the fringe, remove pins as you work to free the plait, rolling the plaited section into a tube; then reposition the plait and hand-stitch it in place, taking a stitch through the plait and a stitch through the robe fabric.

4 Continue rolling and sewing the plait to the seams, allowing the pom-poms to hang freely.

5 At the end, open about 1 inch of the seam, slip the raw end of the plait into the opening, and slip-stitch the opening closed, catching the plait.

6 To decorate the cuffs, position and pin one length of fringe to one cuff, as in Step 1, overlapping the ends at the sleeve seam.

7 To secure the fringe, repeat Steps 2 through 5, then secure the overlap neatly with several stitches.

8 Repeat Steps 6 and 7 for the second cuff.

55

Sanctuary journal

ONE WAY TO REMEMBER the inner journeys made possible in part by your retreats to your personal sanctuary is to keep a journal. The journal does not have to be an expensive book, it just needs to be your designated place to record the revelations that emerge from spending time in your own company. You don't have to write much. As a matter of fact, you can paint or sketch little pictures that represent what you're thinking instead. Buy a blank journal, with rules or not, then make a sensual Ultrasuede jacket to cover it.

materials

Blank book, as desired

2 sheets 8½ × 11–inch cream card stock, or color as desired

¼ yd. cream Ultrasuede (enough to make approximately 2 jackets)

Spray adhesive

Matching thread

Masking tape

You will also need: metal ruler; pencil; X-Acto knife; sewing machine with heavy-duty needle

directions

1 To determine the working measurements for the book jacket, measure and note the dimensions of the blank book as follows: height (A), width (B), and thickness of spine (C).

2 To prepare the liner paper, lay the card stock on a protected work surface.

3 For the cover section, mark and cut one rectangle that measures A + ⅜ inch × B + C + ⅝ inch.

4 For the end flap sections, mark and cut two rectangles, each measuring A + ⅜ inch × 2 ⅜ inches.

5 Lay the Ultrasuede on a work surface, smoothing it flat.

6 To attach the liner paper sections to the Ultrasuede, apply a light coat of spray adhesive to one side of the cover section.

7 Position and press down the cover section, glue side down, on the upper-right-hand corner of the Ultrasuede.

8 Repeat Steps 6 and 7 with the two end flap sections, positioning them to conserve the remaining Ultrasuede for another project.

9 Turn the Ultrasuede over to make certain the fabric is flat and smooth against the paper.
Note: To get rid of wrinkles in the Ultrasuede, lift it off the paper, smooth, and press down again.

10 Turn the Ultrasuede over so the paper faces up.

11 To cut out sections of paper-lined Ultrasuede, place a ruler along each edge of the paper sections, and use an X-Acto knife to make one light cut followed by a second cut until the Ultrasuede is cut through; set the cut-out sections aside.

12 To assemble the jacket, lay the cover section on a work surface, paper side up.

13 Align one end flap along the left outside edge, top and bottom edges even with the cover, Ultrasuede up.
Note: Temporarily secure the end flaps with pieces of masking tape.

14 Repeat Step 13, aligning the remaining end flap along the right outside edge, Ultrasuede up.

15 Machine-stitch around the perimeter of the cover, ⅛ inch from the edges, using 6 to 8 stitches per inch and removing the tape as you work.
Optional: Move the needle manually to round the corners, for neat stitches on the end flaps, and to assist the machine when sewing through thicknesses, if necessary.

16 Slip the covers of the book under the end flap sections and close the cover.

57

Smoothies

ALTHOUGH THERE ARE many ways of treating your outer body so that it glows with health, there are also important ways you can create inner body health and balance. Because stress sets up biochemical changes that can affect your blood chemistry and immune system, you want to invest carefully in your nutrition. The recipes here were inspired by Cherie Calbom and Maureen Keane in *Juicing For Life* and will provide refreshing and healthful drinks to put your body back in balance. You can make these preparations if you have a juicer or a blender.

58

for the juicer

Carrot, Apple, Ginger Juice

4 to 5 carrots (greens removed)

1 apple (cored and seeded)

¼ inch slice ginger root

1 lemon wedge (with peel)

Cantaloupe Ginger Juice

½ cantaloupe (with skin)

¼ inch slice ginger root

Garnish with a sprig of mint

Pineapple, Apple, Cucumber Juice

2 slices pineapple (with skin)

1 apple (cored and seeded)

½ cucumber

1 lemon wedge (with peel)

directions

1

Wash, cut and core fruits and vegetables.

2

Place fruits and vegetables, as indicated, through juicer hopper.

3

Drink juice immediately; pour over ice if desired.

for the blender

Strawberry, Pear, Banana Smoothie

1 pint strawberries (hulled)

½ pear (seeded)

1 banana

½ cup of skim milk

Ice

Cantaloupe Smoothie

½ cantaloupe (remove rind)

¼ to ½ cup of orange juice

Ice

Apple, Grape, Lemon Smoothie

1 apple (cored and seeded)

1 medium bunch of grapes

Juice from 1 lemon wedge

¼ to ½ cup of orange juice

directions

1

Wash, cut and core fruit.

2

Place fruit and liquid ingredients in blender. Turn dial to high. Add ice, if desired.

3

Drink immediately.

59

Etched smoothie glass

LIKE A GLASS from an old-fashioned soda fountain, this smoothie glass is thick-walled and comfortable at the mouth, actually enjoyable to drink from. Vertical bars of glass are separated by narrow channels that give the glass style and provide a secure hold.

You can also use the topography of the glass to your advantage when you design your own etching pattern. Run type down the bars, allowing the channels to guide you in placing the letters. Then consider etching every other bar, again using the channels to help you control the application of the etching cream. Design your own glass for your special recipes and make using it a part of your spa ritual.

materials

60

Drinking glass

High-tack masking tape, ¼ in. wide

Assorted press type, ½-¾ in., as desired

Glass etching cream

Optional

FOR OTHER PATTERNS, AS DESIRED:

for dots: stationary circles, ¼ to ½ in. in diameter

for triangles: self-adhesive Mylar

You will also need: spray glass cleaner; paper towels; scissors; teaspoon; newspaper; rubber gloves; protective eyewear; bristle brush; old toothbrush

directions

Caution: Follow the manufacturer's directions on the etching cream jar, work in a well-ventilated space and wear protective eyewear and rubber gloves.

1
Remove grease and fingerprints from all surfaces of the glass using spray cleaner and paper towels.

2
To apply vertical strips, stretch and press down a length of tape from the bottom to the top, beginning anywhere on the glass; fold over the end of the tape at the rim for easy removal.

3
Lay down a second strip one tape width away from first.

4

Apply four more lengths of tape, as in Steps 2 and 3.

5

To lay down letters, position and press down single letters in a vertical row, a scant ⅛ inch from the last band of tape, spelling out *beauty, healthy,* or another inspiring word. Substitute or add other self-adhesive shapes, as desired

6

Resume taping strips, the next one a scant ⅛ inch from press type.

7

Continue as in Steps 2 and 3, pressing down six strips in all.

8

To etch the glass, pull on rubber gloves and put on protective eyewear.

9

Following the manufacturer's directions, use a bristle brush to apply a coating of etching cream to the exposed surfaces between the strips of tape and over the press type letters, beginning at the bottom and ending at the rim.

10

Wait for the allotted time, approximately 8 to 10 minutes.

11

To remove the cream, hold the glass under running warm water, quickly and carefully using a toothbrush to scrub away the cream and loosen the tape.

12

Peel off any remaining tape and press type; wash the glass in hot, soapy water and dry.

61

Gilded monogram votive

SIMPLE, PERSONAL, and so easy to do, decorating votive candles with letters or other symbols of personal reference is one way we can remind ourselves of our own importance. A small patch of gold is inscribed with a letter of the alphabet, one letter of your monogram.

While the creative experience of gilding the container is in and of itself powerfully restorative of your creativity, inscribing your monogram will be completing a rich spiritual circle. When the candle is lighted, the monogram will glow.

materials

Glass votive candleholder

Quick-dry gold size

2 sheets composition gold leaf

Votive candle

You will also need: glass cleaner; paper towels; masking tape; teaspoon; soft paintbrush; pencil; awl

directions

Caution: Work in a well-ventilated, draft-free space. Do not leave a lighted candle unattended or near flammable materials.

1 Clean the exterior of the votive holder with spray cleaner and paper towels to remove grease and fingerprints.

2 Use strips of masking tape to form a 1¼-inch-wide × ¾-inch-high rectangle centered on one side of the glass.

3 Burnish the edges of the tape, using the bowl of a teaspoon.

4 Apply a thin coat of size within the taped area, allowing the size to dry to tack, about 10 minutes.
Note: A finger touched lightly on the surface will make a tick *sound.*

5 Touch a finger to the gold leaf and pull off a large section, transferring it to the taped-off area of the glass.

6 Tamp the leaf smoothly in place, especially near the edges of the tape, using the eraser end of a pencil.

7 Let the container dry for 48 hours.

8 Use a soft paintbrush to remove extra flakes of leaf, then carefully peel off the tape to reveal the gilded section.

9 Use an awl to freehand write an initial in the gilded rectangle.
Note: The letter will be faint but will appear more prominent when the candle is lighted.

63

Eye pillow

TO SOOTHE YOUR EYES and alleviate puffiness, make this little eye pillow from a scrap of the softest brushed silk. The pillow is filled with lavender buds, allowing it to conform to the contours of your eyes and nose.

materials

9 × 8–in. rectangle brushed silk

½ in. wide Velcro tape, 3⅛ in. long

Matching thread

1 cup lavender buds

You will also need: straight pins; scissors; sewing machine

directions

Caution: Do not use if you have allergies to lavender.

64

1 Fold a ⅜-inch hem on one 8-inch side of the silk rectangle.

2 Lay the rectangle hem side up on a flat work surface.

3 Separate the Velcro tape and center the loop section of the Velcro over the hem on the left side of the rectangle and the hook section over the opposite side, with the edges of the strips slightly lower than the folded edge of the silk; pin the strips in place.

4 Stitch down the Velcro strips around all sides, a scant ⅛ inch from the edges.

5 Fold the rectangle in half lengthwise, right sides facing, all edges even, using pins to secure.

6 Machine-stitch the two long sides and the bottom short side, ⅜ inch from the edges, removing pins as you work.

7 Turn the pillow right side out and fill half full with lavender buds and press the Velcro strips together.

Hand-molded soaps

THOUGH IT SOUNDS unromantic to use leftover slivers from worn-down soaps, this is not only a resourceful way to recycle material that might otherwise go to waste but the symbolic "ore" that can alchemically change into gold—those emollient soap balls that you would have to spend a lot for if you bought them in a store.

You can make simple soap by recycling and in so doing avoid the process often associated with making soap from scratch—cauldrons boiling over with foam and toxic vapors. Although this is an exaggeration, there is a way to be practical and self-indulgent at the same time. You can reconstitute leftover soap bars and slivers by adding olive oil, then hand-molding soothing oil soaps. You can add any scent you desire, using ground herbs or a few drops of fragrance oil. The soaps are sensual to use, fitting in your cupped hands, and the benefits of their natural ingredients will be felt in smooth skin.

materials

10 oz. soap ends, bits and pieces of used bars (or bars, as desired, to make up 10 oz.)

8 to 9 tbsp. olive oil

3 drops essential oil*, as desired (see the chart on pages 106-107)

*Caution: *Before using an essential oil, be sure to follow the health cautions contained on the copyright page iv.*

You will also need: hand-held cheese grater; plastic cutting board; heavy pot; wooden spoon; stainless steel measuring spoons; rubber gloves; wax paper

Do not use any equipment with copper, aluminum, cast-iron or Teflon finishes.

directions

1
To prepare the soap slivers, finely grate all the soap onto cutting board, transferring the piles to a pot as you work.

2
Use a measuring spoon to add the olive oil to the pot.

3
Place the pot over a stove burner, turn the heat to high, and stir the mixture constantly until it is "cookie dough" consistency, adding a few drops of olive oil if necessary.

4
When the soap is doughy and slightly mealy, remove it from the heat.

5
Mix in the essential oil with a spoon, cleaning with alcohol when finished, followed by wash in hot-soapy water.

6
Pull on rubber gloves, and apply and distribute a drop of olive oil to the palms.

7
Scoop out a clump of soap, packing and shaping it like a snowball; set the ball on wax paper; repeat. Allow the soap to harden overnight.

65

Oil lamps

ALTHOUGH NOT BRIGHT ENOUGH to illuminate your entire vanity area, oil lamps, nonetheless, can create just the right mood in your sanctuary. With their soft flickering flames, oil lamps are romantic accents that are deceivingly easy to make; all you need is a pretty bottle, some lamp oil, a length of cotton wick, and a glass bead. Oil lamps tend to be long burning because the oil provides a steady supply of fuel for the flame.

materials

Two 10-oz. sturdy glass bottles with ⅛-in. to 3⁄16-in. thick walls

Lamp oil, approximately 16 fl. oz. (8 oz. for each bottle)

2 glass beads, each with a hole for a wick, and each slightly larger in diameter than the bottle neck opening

You will also need: ruler; scissors; pencil; and tweezers.

Caution: Never leave a lighted oil lamp unattended; keep it away from flammable materials and children.

directions

Caution: When the wick is lighted, the bead gets hot. Use tweezers to adjust the length of the wick to keep the flame burning, if necessary. Wait until the bead cools before adjusting the level of oil.

67

1
To prepare bottles, wash in hot soapy water; let dry.

2
To prepare one wick, use a ruler to measure the height of one bottle from base to rim, adding 2 inches; repeat for second bottle.

3
Use scissors to cut the wick to the measurement taken in Step 2; repeat for the second wick.

4
Pour lamp oil into each bottle to within 1½ inches of the top rim.

5
To prime the wicks, soak each wick in oil, running your fingers along the wick to get rid of any excess.

6
Thread one end of one wick through the hole in one bead, leaving ¾ inch above the hole.

7
Place the threaded bead on a protected work surface, and carefully tie the opposite end of the wick in a loose knot.

8
To position the beaded wick on the bottle, guide the knotted end of the wick into the bottle, using a pencil, and allow the bead to rest on the rim of the bottle neck, the wick extended above the hole.

9
To make the second oil lamp, repeat Steps 6 through 8.

10
Position the oil lamps on a level surface and use a match to light the wicks.

Jeweled and etched oil decanter

WHEN YOU ARE SEEKING containers for your bath and body care preparations, do not overlook the kitchen departments of large department or specialty stores. Sturdy, well-designed glassware will be available at every turn. From squatty glass jars with metal dispenser lids like those used to shake out grated cheese to beaker-style bottles with pretty glass ball stoppers like those used to dispense olive oil and tinted and frosted vials, many containers are adaptable for use in your home spa preparations. The value of glass is that it is not porous and therefore maintains the potency of the concoction inside much longer.

materials

New glass decanter with glass stopper

Masking tape

Glass etching cream

1 green glass cabochon

5-Minute Epoxy

You will also need: teaspoon; bristle brush; protective eyewear; rubber gloves; scrap cardboard; toothpicks

directions

Caution: Follow the manufacturer's directions on the etching cream jar; work in a well-ventilated space; wear rubber gloves and protective eyewear. When you are ready to fill your containers, it is very important that you sterilize them in a solution of ¼ cup household bleach and 1 gallon of water. Boil for 20 minutes and let them airdry.

1
To mark your etched design, press a length of masking tape around the decanter, approximately 5 inches above the bottom, burnishing the edges with the bowl of a teaspoon.

2
Etch the section above the tape, following the directions on page 61, steps 8-12.

3
Affix the cabochon below the spout, ½ inch above the line of etching, following the directions on page 75, step 5.

Gilded bottle stopper with label

SIMPLE ACCENTS CAN be enough to add luxury and a sense of self-indulgence to any object. The stopper on an apothecary-style bottle is the perfect place to add an elegant detail like gold leaf. This bottle is pictured on page 95.

materials

New glass apothecary-style bottle with stopper

Quick-dry gold size

1 sheet composition gold leaf

Epoxy sealer

You will also need: glass cleaner; paper towels; ¾-in. bristle brush; mineral spirits; cotton ball; large mixing bowl

directions

Caution: Work in a well-ventilated, draft-free space.

1 Clean the stopper with spray cleaner and paper towels to remove grease and fingerprints.

2 On a protected work surface, brush a thin coat of size on the top and rim of the stopper, avoiding the stem; stand the stopper upright.

3 Allow the size to reach tack, about 10 to 13 minutes.
Note: A finger touched lightly on the surface will make a tick *sound.*

4 Lay the sheet of gold leaf on a flat surface, tear off uneven ½-inch pieces, and apply them to the sized surfaces, using a finger until the surfaces are covered.

5 Use the eraser end of a pencil to tamp down leaf; let the stopper dry overnight.

6 Lightly brush a cotton ball over the gilded surfaces to remove any gold flakes and use to burnish the leaf.

7 Apply a light coat of sealer, following the manufacturer's directions and let dry 48 hours; replace stopper in the bottle.

69

Poetry.

Poetry carries its own Conviction
with it, and has native Beauty enough
to silence all its Opposers, and dazzle the ...
with over powering Lustre, ...
... it spreads a ...
and undesignedly betrays its own ...

... earning is Silver in the Hands of Common
People, Gold in those of Noble Descent, but
... amonds in the Hands of Princes ...

Etched carafe and tumbler

REMINISCENT OF THE sleek sophistication of the 1930s, this coordinated carafe and tumbler set looks like it came straight from a grand Hollywood home. The narrow frosty stripes that encircle the base and neck of the carafe are offset by strict and slender stripes etched vertically on the tumbler. When the two pieces are together, the way they were designed to be stored, they are a picture of elegance.

The carafe can be filled and the tumbler inverted over its mouth to keep dust out. And the mouth of the carafe is a safe and convenient resting place for the tumbler. When filled with your most healthful drink, the carafe can be placed on your tubside table, or it can be put beside you bed and filled with cool mineral water dashed with a sprig of mint, ready to baptize you into sleeping and dreaming. Either way, you will love the morning or evening ritual of preparing your daily drink in these beautiful vessels.

materials

New glass carafe

New tumbler that fits over neck of
  carafe, if desired

High-tack masking tape, ½ in. wide

Pinstripe tape, ⅛ in. wide

Glass etching cream

You will also need: spray glass cleaner; paper towels; ruler; plain paper; teaspoon; newspaper; rubber gloves; protective eyewear; paintbrush, ¼ in. wide; old toothbrush

Etched carafe and tumbler
directions

Caution: Follow the manufacturer's directions on the etching cream jar, work in a well-ventilated space, and wear protective eyewear and rubber gloves.

1
Remove grease and fingerprints from all surfaces of the carafe and tumbler using spray cleaner and paper towels.

2
To mark the beginning of the horizontal stripe design at the bottom and neck sections on the carafe, use the ruler and masking tape to measure and mark a line 1⅛ inches from the bottom edge and a second line 1⅛ inches from the top rim, pressing the tape down all around and neatly overlapping the ends.
Note: These strips will identify the position of the first pinstripes at the bottom and top of the carafe.

3
To lay down the pinstripe tape on the bottom section of the carafe, press down the end of the tape on the glass, adjacent to the top edge of the masking tape, and press down the tape all around, neatly overlapping the ends.

4
Lay down a second horizontal strip, one tape width away from the first; then lay down four more parallel strips, each one pinstripe width away from the previously laid strip.

5
To lay down the pinstripe tape on the neck of the carafe, apply four strips just under the masking tape, as in Steps 3 and 4, working downward. Set the carafe aside.

6
To mark the beginning of the vertical stripe design on the tumbler, position and apply one strip of masking tape perpendicular to the lip, beginning anywhere on the circumference, pressing one end of the tape to the lip and the other to the base.

7

To lay down pinstripes, position and press down thirteen strips of tape, all ⅛ inch apart, perpendicular to the rim of the tumbler.

8

When all the tape is laid down on all sections of the carafe and tumbler, apply a sheet of plain paper over the strips, one section at a time, using the bowl of the teaspoon to burnish the edges of the tape. *Note: This will assure clean lines when the etching cream is applied.*

9

To protect glass surfaces that are not to be etched, mask areas adjacent to the taped design using overlapping lengths of masking tape.

10

Cover your work surface with newspaper, pull on rubber gloves, and put on protective eyewear.

11

To etch the pinstripes on the carafe, use a paintbrush to apply a coating of etching cream to the exposed surfaces between the strips of tape, beginning at the bottom and ending at the neck. Set the carafe aside.

12

Repeat Step 13 to etch the pinstripes on the tumbler.

73

13

Allow the cream to work for approximately 12 to 15 minutes, or as instructed on the jar.

14

To remove the cream, hold the carafe under warm running water, quickly and carefully using a toothbrush to scrub away the cream and loosen the tape. Wash the carafe in hot, soapy water and dry.

15

Repeat Step 14 for the tumbler.

Jeweled pitcher and tumbler

SOMETIMES THE MOST beautiful things are the most simple. Here the addition of sparkling drops of green glass adds just the right detail to the bowl of a pitcher and the belly of a stout tumbler.

Taking only a short time to decorate, each plain glass object was made more attractive with the addition of these precious-looking stones in a cabochon style. The secret to this decoration is 5-minute epoxy, which allows you to glue two nonporous items together. Just keep in mind that the process creates a near-indestructible bond, so be pretty sure you want to add such permanent decoration.

materials

New glass pitcher

New glass tumbler

Masking tape

11 green glass cabochons

5-Minute Epoxy

You will also need: spray glass cleaner; paper towels; towels; pencil; rubber gloves; protective eyewear; scrap cardboard; toothpicks

directions

Caution: Work in a well-ventilated room, and wear rubber gloves and protective eyewear. Follow the manufacturer's directions carefully.

1 Clean the pitcher and tumbler with spray cleaner and paper towels to remove grease and fingerprints.

2 Lay the pitcher on its side on a protected work surface, bolstering the sides with wadded up towels to stabilize it; do the same for the tumbler.

3 To mark the horizontal band of cabochons, center a 7-inch length of masking tape around the front of the pitcher (under the spout), 5 inches from the bottom.

4 Mark on the tape seven points, ⅞ inch apart.
Note: These points indicate the position of the center of one cabochon.

5 Mix the 5-minute epoxy following the manufacturer's directions on a scrap of cardboard. When the glue is runny, dab it with a toothpick to transfer a small blob to the back of a cabochon, immediately centering and pressing the stone to the glass just above a mark on the tape.

6 Wait until the glue sets before adding the next stone to prevent the stones from sliding out of position.

7 Repeat Steps 5 and 6 for each remaining stones.

8 Center a 4-inch band of masking tape on the front of the tumbler 2 inches above the bottom.

9 Mark on the tape four points, ⅞ inch apart.

10 Repeat Steps 5 through 7.

11 Let the epoxy cure 1 hour, then remove the tape, wash the pitcher and tumbler in hot, soapy water, and dry.

Soap purse

KEEPING YOUR FRAGRANT cakes of soap in elegant purses until you are ready to use them is one way of taking part in the ceremony of caring for yourself. If you make your own soap, you will probably make more than you can use at one time. Consider stitching several purses in which to put the extra soap, storing some and giving some as gifts.

These little purses can be made in any fancy fabric, and you can accent the edges with beads sewn in clusters. Slip a cake or two inside each purse, and store the purse in your linen closet or lingerie drawer. It will infuse those spaces with the scent of the soap.

materials

4½ × 10–inch rectangle green crinkled
  silk organza

Matching thread

½ yd. silk cord

Optional

3-in. green silk tassel

Glass seed beads in gold and moss
  green

You will also need: straight pins;
sewing machine with buttonhole foot
and zigzag capability; safety pin; hand-
sewing and beading needles; scissors

directions

1
Lay the fabric rectangle lengthwise, right
side up, on a flat work surface.

2
Fold the rectangle in half, bringing the
bottom short side up to meet the top
short side, pinning, then machine-stitching
the sides.

3
Measure and mark the midpoint of the
bottom edge with a straight pin.

4
Measure and mark points 1½ inches above
the bottom edge at each side.

5
To create the point of the purse, connect
the midpoint on the bottom edge to each
marked side, using machine-stitching to
secure and removing the pins as you work.

6
Trim the seam allowance to ¼ inch around
the point.

7
To create the cord casing, double-fold and
press ¼ inch, then ¾ inch at the top edge.

8
Open the folds and machine-stitch the raw
edge, using a zigzag stitch.

9
To create eyelets for the cord, mark and
sew two ⅜–inch buttonholes, one at the
center front and the other at the center
back of the casing, ½ inch from the edge.

10
Refold the casing, topstitching it in place
along the fold.

11
Attach a safety pin to one end of the cord
and insert it into the front buttonhole in
the casing and exit out the second button
hole, securing the ends of the cord with a
double knot.

12
Optional: To decorate the point of the
purse, pick open several stitches at the
point, inserting the hanging loop from the
a tassel; torn purse to wrong side and
restitch the point using a sewing machine.

13
Turn the purse right side out and hand-
stitch the seed beads in clusters of three to
both sides of the point.

Vanity tray

A VANITY TRAY can be one of the most convenient and practical ways of holding and organizing your often-used skin and body preparations while adding a touch of elegance to your vanity area. The tray can also protect your counters or tables from the unavoidable spills. If anything spills on the glass surface of the tray, use a damp cloth to wipe it up—no permanent stains to worry about.

The vanity tray is deceivingly easy to make from a recycled picture frame. All you do is decorate the glass using a pretty illustration, gilding the border with gold leaf. Four little ball feet are added to lift the frame and form a pedestal-style tray. You can make several trays, each in a different size, and use them as portable beauty centers or keepers of other beauty accessories, like combs, brushes, or perfumes.

materials

Ornate picture frame, or as desired

Illustration from calendar, gift wrap, greeting card, or as desired

ModPodge™ decoupage glue

Quick-dry size

Black acrylic paint

Black mat board, equal in size to the back of the frame

4 wooden balls, ⅞ inch diameter

Contact cement

5-Minute Epoxy

You will also need: spray glass cleaner; paper towels; ruler; X-Acto knife; 2 sponge brushes; cloth; rubber gloves; mineral spirits; scrap cardboard, cotton swab

directions

Caution: Work in a well-ventilated, draft-free space and wear rubber gloves.

1 Dismantle the frame, removing the back and separating the glass from the frame. *Note: If the frame backing has an easel stand, carefully remove it to create a flat back.*

2 Clean the glass with spray cleaner and paper towels to remove grease and fingerprints; then lay the glass on a protected work surface.

3 To prepare the center illustration, use a ruler and X-Acto knife to measure and cut a rectangle from the art that is approximately 1¼ inches smaller than frame's opening measurement, selecting a pleasing portion of the art, as desired.

4 Use a sponge brush to apply a thin, even coat of ModPodge™ to the front and edges of the illustration.

5 Center the illustration on the glass, glue side down, and tap it gently in place.

6 Flip the glass over to view the illustration, adjusting its position if necessary.

7 Turn the glass back over and smooth the illustration firmly in place with your fingers, working any excess glue out from under the image with a damp cloth.

8 Lay the glass on a protected work surface, wrong side of the illustration facing up, and brush a thin, even coat of size on the exposed glass surfaces, including a ¼-inch border of the illustration.

9 Lay one full sheet of gold leaf on any sized portion of the glass, tapping it gently in place.

10 Continue applying sheets of leaf to the remaining sized areas of glass, allowing the leaf to overlap; wait 5 minutes.

11 To create a crackle pattern in the leaf, pull on rubber gloves and use a finger to firmly press down, breaking the surface of the leaf.

12 Continue pressing down on the leaf with your finger, creating an all-over random crackle pattern.
Note: Turn the glass over to front to check the developing pattern; if dissatisfied, or if breaks are too gaping, reapply smaller pieces of leaf to cover any unwanted gaps.

13 When you are satisfied with the crackle pattern, let size dry completely, about 48 hours.

14 When the size is completely dry, use a dry sponge brush to remove extra gold leaf, saving big pieces for future projects.

15 Use a clean brush to apply black paint to the glass, covering the illustration and all gilded surfaces; let the paint dry.

16 Apply a second coat of paint; let it dry.

17 To protect the surfaces, apply two coats of clear acrylic sealer, allowing the first coat to dry before applying the second.

18 Reposition the glass in the frame, illustration side out, followed by the backing.

19 To seal the back of the frame, apply contact cement to a ¼-inch border around all sides of the mat board, positioning the board carefully over the frame's backing and pressing down to secure.

20 Turn the frame to the back, and, following the manufacturer's directions, mix up a small amount of epoxy on scrap of cardboard, waiting until glue is no longer runny to dab a blob onto each corner of the frame using a cotton swab.

21 Immediately set a ball in the glue at one corner, allowing the glue to set up, about 5 minutes.

22 Repeat Step 21 to attach the remaining three feet; allow the epoxy to cure.

Hand towels with ribbon accents

PERFECT FOR DRYING your hands, these towels are also perfect for using on your face, after a rose-water splash. Make a stack to serve your hands and another to reserve for your morning face rituals.

materials

2 white linen hand towels

Grosgrain ribbon:

approximately 1 yd.* with black-and-white stripes, ½ inch wide

approximately 1 yd.* magenta, ⅜ inch wide

Matching thread

You will also need: ruler; scissors; straight pins; sewing machine

directions

1
Lay one towel lengthwise and right side up on a flat work surface.

*
2
Measure and cut two lengths of the black-and-white ribbon, each equal to the width of the towel plus ¾ inch; repeat with the magenta ribbon.

3
Fold and press a ⅜-inch hem at each end of each black-and-white ribbon; repeat for the magenta ribbons.

4
Center one length of the black-and-white ribbon across the towel, approximately 1¼ inches above the bottom edge of the towel, using straight pins to secure it; topstitch the ribbon in place a scant ⅛ inch from all ribbon edges.

5
Center one length of the magenta ribbon across the towel, with the bottom edge touching the top edge of the black-and-white ribbon, using straight pins to secure it; topstitch the ribbon in place a scant ⅛ inch from all ribbon edges.

6
To decorate the opposite end of the towel, repeat Steps 4 and 5.

81

sustaining the benefits of
your spa
experience

Be alert to those brief moments during the day

when you experience your fundamental self

behind a breath, a feeling, a sensation.

—Deepak Chopra

YOU WILL FIND that your body and spirit naturally carry the beneficial effects of your bathing experiences and their attendant gifts for some time. But predictably, some effects will fade as your hectic daily life intervenes and draws your attention to other concerns.

83

Fortunately, you can sustain many of the benefits of your spa experience without installing the entire regimen in your daily routine. One way to do this is to reinforce the links previously established while in your home spa by bringing a level of intimate awareness to whatever ministration you do, however simple.

To get in touch with your senses and yourself as you practice your shorter, daily beauty and self care routines, pay close attention to what you are doing and how you are feeling. Prepare and apply a facial mask customized to your particular skin type. Breathe in the herbal essences of your facial splash as you mist your face and body. Listen to the same music you heard in your home spa while you smooth lotion on your feet.

You will find that these mindful practices will invoke the mind-body connections first experienced when you were in your personal sanctuary and they will help lead you back to the timeless you.

Hand care

TOO MUCH TIME in the sun, cold weather and frequent washing can all cause rough, dry skin. This simple remedy will help to heal your hands and restore their natural beauty.

materials

YIELD: ONE TREATMENT

1 tsp. honey

1 tsp. olive oil

stainless steel measuring spoons

glass bowl

disposable gloves

directions

1 Combine honey and olive oil in glass bowl.

2 Massage mixture into your hands.

3 Put on disposable gloves and wait 20 minutes.

4 Rinse hands with warm water.

84

Foot care

THIS MIXTURE WILL SOOTHE, cool and moisturize the most tired of feet.

materials

YIELD: ONE TREATMENT

5 tbsp. aloe vera gel

¼ tbsp. peppermint oil

¼ tbsp. eucalyptus oil

glass bowl

stainless steel measuring spoons

stainless steel whisk

directions

1 Combine aloe vera gel that has been refrigerated with essential oils in glass bowl. Use whisk to mix.

2 Rub on feet until absorbed.

Eye care

SOOTHING PUFFY, tired eyes requires little more than a trip to your refrigerator and 10 minutes to spare. You will see and feel the difference it makes.

materials

YIELD: ONE TREATMENT

4 thin slices of cucumber or potato

distilled water

stainless steel knife

cutting board

spray bottle

directions

1
Cut 4 thin slices of cucumber or potato.

2
Spritz eye area with distilled water.

3
Place one slice on each eye for 5 minutes.

4
Repeat with 2 new slices for an additional 5 minutes.

Hot oil hair treatment

DEEP-CONDITIONING your hair with hot oil will leave it shiny and manageable. If you have normal hair, use olive oil. For oily hair use sesame oil, and for dry hair, jojoba oil.

ingredients

1 oz. olive oil

Essential oils*:

5 drops rosemary oil

5 drops peppermint oil

Rubbing alcohol

*Caution: *Before using an essential oil, be sure to follow the health cautions contained on the copyright page iv.*

You will also need: glass measuring cup; eyedropper; stainless steel or enamel double boiler; stainless steel spoon; small bowl or saucer; shower cap; towel

Do not use any equipment with copper, aluminum, cast-iron or Teflon finishes.

directions

1
Measure and mix olive and essential oils in the top of double boiler, warming mixture over very low heat and watching constantly.

2
To test oil temperature, stir with spoon, then lift spoon and allow a drop of oil to fall on your palm; if oil is warm, it is ready.

3
Pour oil into small bowl or saucer, then drizzle into one palm; rub palms together and massage oil into scalp and through wet hair; cover head with shower cap to retain heat and facilitate absorption.

4
Wrap towel around head.

5
Wait 15 minutes, then remove towel and shampoo hair, if desired.

6
Bowls, spoons, etc. can be cleaned with rubbing alcohol first to cut the oil, then warm soapy water.

Scented body splashes

BODY SPLASHES CAN be used as light perfume or as mild deodorant. They are easy and inexpensive to make, and they are toning and refreshing to the skin. Basically, body splashes are made with distilled water and essential oils. But unless they are used immediately or made up in small batches, it is wise to add some alcohol, like vodka, to retard the natural growth of bacteria. For extra measure, store your splashes in the refrigerator.

When you are ready to dispense your splash after a warm shower, bath, or exercise session, use a spray bottle to lightly mist your skin. You can also pour the splash into your cupped hand and splash it over your body in more generous amounts. In any case, the cool, light fragrance will be so invigorating! Be aware that citrus oils can cause photosensitivity. Do not expose skin to sun after use.

ingredients

YIELD: 14 OZ.

For Base:

12 oz. distilled water

2 oz. vodka

Rubbing alcohol

For Fragrance Blends

Invigorating Citrus Blend:

Base for splash

Essential oils*:

10 drops grapefruit oil

5 drops cypress oil

2 drops lemon oil

Relaxing Sensual Blend:

Base for splash

Essential oils*:

5 drops lavender oil

3 drops vanilla oil

3 drops frankincense oil

3 drops myrrh

Soothing Floral Blend:

Base for splash

Essential oils*:

10 drops sandalwood oil

3 drops mandarin orange oil

*Caution: *Before using an essential oil, be sure to follow the health cautions contained on the copyright page iv.*

You will also need: 16-oz. plastic spray bottle; glass measuring cup; stainless steel funnel; glass eyedropper

Do not use any equipment with copper, aluminum, cast-iron or Teflon finishes.

directions

1 To make base, measure and pour distilled water through funnel into spray bottle; repeat with vodka.

2 Add essential oil. Clean eyedropper with rubbing alcohol.

3 Secure spray top and shake well before using.

87

Decorative glycerin soaps

IT IS EASY to make your own glycerin soaps and provide just the aromatherapeutic benefits you need by adding an herbal scent or essential oil. You will love the actual procedure because in it you will see the transformation of colorless molten soap to gleaming bars in pastel colors. Once the soap is hard, you can inscribe the surface with words that have symbolic meaning in your life.

Here are the essentials of making any molded soap and some interesting variations.

Molded soap

materials

Note: You can use this recipe to make one large block of soap, cutting slices one at a time as needed.

YIELD: APPROXIMATELY TEN 4-OZ. BAR SOAPS OR SIXTEEN 2½-OZ. ROUND CAKES

Plastic molds:

For bar soap: 3¼ in. long × 2¼ in. wide × 1⅛ in. deep

For round cakes: 2½-in. diameter and 1 in. deep

Vegetable oil

2½ lb. clear, unscented glycerin soap

Liquid food color or soap-making color:

Approximately less than one drop to scant smear

Essential oil*, as desired:

Approximately 1 tsp. for 2½ lb. soap

Caution: Before using an essential oil, be sure to follow the health cautions contained on the copyright page iv.

Optional

For large block, use narrow loaf pan or ceramic dish

You will also need: cutting board; sharp knife; 2 microwave-safe containers with spouts and handles; plastic wrap; access to microwave oven; saucer; spoon; fork; measuring spoon; wooden skewer

basic directions

1
Apply a light coating of vegetable oil to the interior of the mold, using your finger.

2
On a cutting board, cut the slab of glycerin soap in half, then into small chunks.

3
Place half the chunks in one microwave-safe container and the remainder in the second container; cover each container with plastic wrap.

4
Put one container in a microwave oven and heat for 20 seconds, then 10 seconds, then 5 seconds, stirring and checking to see if the soap has liquefied.

5
When the soap is liquid, remove the container from the microwave.

6
To add color, squeeze 1 drop of chosen food coloring on a saucer, then dip in one tine of a fork to collect a scant bit of color, stirring the soap with the fork to blend in the color.
Note: Add color sparingly for a more subtle pastel shade.

7
To add scent, use a measuring spoon to add ¼ teaspoon of essential oil, stirring gently with the fork to blend.

8
Immediately pour the soap into the pre-pared molds, stopping ¼ inch from the top rim; allow the soap to set undisturbed until it is firm, approximately 30 minutes.
Note: The soap will begin to develop a skin quickly; use a wooden skewer to skim the skin off the surface, or block the skin with a spoon as you pour the soap into the mold.

9
Repeat Steps 3 through 8 to melt, color and scent, and mold the remaining soap, changing the color and fragrance as desired; or make the design variations on the following page.

10
Turn the mold over, hitting it hard against a protected work surface.
Note: The soap should fall out of the mold, but if it does not, put the mold into the freezer for 5 minutes, then remove it and repeat Step 10.

89

design variations

Layered Color: Tint two batches of melted soap different colors. Pour one color into a mold halfway to the rim, allowing that layer to set; then add a second layer of soap in a second color, stopping ¼ inch from the rim of the mold.

Floral: Pour soap into the mold halfway to the rim; then gently lay pressed silk or fresh flowers and foliage in a pattern on the surface, allowing the soap to set; melt and pour a second layer of clear soap, stopping ¼ inch from the rim of the mold.

Decoupage: Cut an illustration from gift wrap or some other source; follow the directions for floral, substituting the illustration for flowers.

Objects: Follow the directions for floral, using a small object instead, and using clear soap throughout so the object can be seen.

Layered Herbs: Follow the directions for layered color, adding dried herbs, like lavender or thyme, as desired, to the first batch of soap; color each batch a separate but coordinating color, grating in lemon rind or the rind of some other citrus fruit.

Inscribed: Follow the basic directions, inscribing a word or saying, like *peace* or *soul*, with a pointed skewer; gently center and inscribe the word into the top surface of the soap, removing soap to a depth of ⅛ inch; add curlicues and serifs or other accents to the letters as desired.

90

Hand-shaped soap

materials

As above except:

substitute Teflon cookie sheet for plastic molds

You will also need: wrapped stub wire; ruler, sharp pencil, or wooden skewer; leaf pattern

basic directions

1 To prepare the cookie sheet, smooth it with a light coat of oil.

2 Follow the basic directions for melting soap described in Steps 1 through 4 on page 88-89, melting all the soap at one time in a larger microwave-safe container with spout and handle.

3 When the soap is melted, color it apple green by adding ½ drop of green and 1 drop of yellow, blending the color with a skewer.
Note: For darker green, omit the yellow, adding 1 full drop of green to the melted soap.

4 Add 1 teaspoon of chosen scent, blending again.

5
Lift the container and steadily pour ⅛-inch layer of melted soap on the surface of the cookie sheet, tilting the sheet for full coverage of all stem wire.
Note: Do not move the cookie sheet once the soap has been poured, and push any bubbles on the surface to the sides of sheet with the skewer.

6
Allow the soap to set undisturbed until it is firm, approximately 20 minutes.
Note: To test, pry up one corner; it should lift off the sheet easily.

7
When the soap is set, lay a leaf pattern over one wire stem, aligning the marked stem of the leaf with the wire.

8
Use a skewer or knife to trace around the leaf shape, pressing hard enough to cut through the full thickness of soap but not so hard you damage the Teflon.

9
Lift off the leaf pattern and repeat Step 8 for the remaining leaves.

10
To remove the soap leaf from the sheet, pry up one end of the leaf, using a skewer; then gently lift the entire leaf, supporting the wired area to avoid tearing; set the leaf aside.

11
Repeat Step 10 for the remaining leaves.

12
To create veins on each leaf, lay the leaf on a flat work surface and use a skewer or the tip of a knife to freehand draw scratches in forked patterns on the top surface of the soap, using a fresh leaf or a silk leaf as a guide.
Note: Do not cut through the soap.

13
Repeat Step 12 for the remaining leaves.

14
Hold a leaf with both hands at opposite ends and use your thumbs to smooth, bend, and undulate the soap into a natural-looking shape.

15
Display the leaves in a soap dish, or as desired.

16
Collect the unused sections of soap, trying the ringlet design variation.

91

Exfoliation

EXFOLIATING YOUR SKIN helps to remove any dirt, oil, or dead skin that may be blocking your pores; therefore, this natural abrasive procedure makes your body more efficient at eliminating toxins.

Exfoliating also increases your circulation and creates a healthy glow on your skin. You can exfoliate before showering, known as dry brushing, or you can exfoliate during your shower. The procedure is the same. Holding some slightly rough cloth or brush, scrub your extremities first, working in a circular motion in the direction of your heart. Be cautious around sensitive areas such as your neck and breasts.

Here are a variety of products in different fibers that you can use to exfoliate your body.

Loofah: Really a member of the cucumber family, a whole loofah "sponge" can be held in the hand and used au naturel; or it can be attached to a hand mitt or a long handle. The long-handled version is perfect for exfoliating hard-to-reach places, like your back.

Natural Bristle Brush: Available in a variety of sizes, natural bristle brushes can be placed in your hand or have long handles. The quality of the bristles is important and should be compatible with the skin you are using them on. Face brushes are usually smaller with softer bristles. The bristles on body brushes are typically stiffer.

Sisal Fiber: Sisal is a natural fiber obtained from the leaves of the agave plant; slightly rough and strong, it is woven into mitts, washcloths, or backstraps.

Silk: Fine, soft, and shiny, raw silk is woven to create mitts and washcloths that are gentle on the skin, especially sensitive skin.

Pumice Stone: A light, porous volcanic rock, pumice has a visible cellular structure, is lightweight, and floats. Pumice should be used only to exfoliate dry skin on callused feet, and then it should be accompanied by superfatted soap or body oil to avoid its drying effects.

93

Facial scrub

FACIAL SCRUBS ARE great ways to remove dead skin cells, improve circulation, tighten pores, and moisturize the skin. Composed of a particulate substance, like ground nuts, and a creamy ingredient that holds the ground material together, facial scrubs gently help the skin slough off dirt and dead skin cells. Facial scrubs can be used every one to two weeks, depending on your skin condition.

94

ingredients

YIELD: ENOUGH FOR ONE TREATMENT

1½-2 tbsp. rolled oats (ground)

1½ tsp. almonds (ground)

1-1½ tbsp. honey

½ medium apple (peeled, cored, and chopped)

You will also need: coffee grinder; mixing bowl and spoon; measuring spoons; knife; cutting board; blender or food processor; storage jar

directions

1

Clean grinder very well and use to grind rolled oats, leaving some grit; store in bowl.

2

Repeat Step 1 to grind almonds, leaving some grit; store in bowl.

3

To make honey and apple paste, cut apple into pieces; measure and place ingredients in blender or food processor, blending until smooth.

4

Fold paste into oats and almonds, using spoon to mix. If mixture is too wet, add more ground oats; if it is too dry, add more honey.

5

When thoroughly mixed, spoon paste into jar.

6

When ready to use, gently rub paste onto face in a circular motion for 3 to 5 minutes.

7

Rinse with warm water and gently pat skin dry.

Face splash

ESSENTIAL OILS CAN do wonderful things for your skin, whether it is dry, normal, or oily. These face splashes combine water and oils and act to calm and restore the natural balance of the skin. They can help soothe and repair some skin damage, as well as reduce some common skin problems. Use these preparations to tone your skin after you have washed your face. They can be followed by makeup or your moisturizer. Be aware that citrus oils can cause photosensitivity. Do not expose skin to sun after use. Avoid contact with eye area.

Normal Skin: Lavender oil, peppermint oil

Dry Skin: Fennel oil, sandalwood oil

Oily Skin: Grapefruit, lemongrass, or other citrus oil

Irritated Skin: Chamomile oil, lavender oil

Acne-Prone Skin: Rosemary, tea tree, or sage oil

ingredients

1 oz. distilled water

5 drops of essential oil*

Rubbing alcohol

*Caution: *Before using an essential oil, be sure to follow the health cautions contained on the copyright page iv.*

You will also need: glass measuring cup with ounce demarcations; stainless steel measuring spoons; eyedropper; clear spray bottle

Do not use any equipment with copper, aluminum, cast-iron or Teflon finishes.

directions

1 Measure water and essential oil, placing ingredients directly into spray bottle. Clean eyedropper with rubbing alcohol.

2 Secure bottle tightly and shake to blend ingredients.

3 To dispense, spray splash directly on face or use cotton balls, soaking, then blotting on face, as desired.

4 Store bottle in refrigerator.

95

Face masks

OF COURSE THE BEST way to have great skin is to begin on the inside, drinking plenty of water and eating a balanced diet. Another way to ensure good skin is to combine natural ingredients to nourish and repair your skin. Face masks can remove dead, dry skin cells, moisturize, rejuvenate, heal or repair, depending on your skin type and the ingredients you choose. Not only are face masks relaxing but incorporating them into your regular routine will produce visible benefits. In order not to strip your face of all its natural oils, masks should only be used once or twice a week.

96

Mask for normal skin

ingredients

YIELD: ONE APPLICATION

1½ tsp. honey

3 to 5 drops of lavender essential oil*

Rubbing alcohol

*Caution: *Before using an essential oil, be sure to follow the health cautions contained on the copyright page iv.*

You will also need: glass bowl; stainless steel measuring spoon; eyedropper

directions

1

Combine honey and lavender oil in bowl. Clean eyedropper by using rubbing alcohol to remove the oil.

2

Apply to face. Avoid eye area. Leave on for 20 minutes.

3

Rinse with warm water. Pat face dry.

Caution: Do not use any equipment with copper, aluminum, cast iron or Teflon finishes.

Mask for dry skin

ingredients

YIELD: ONE TO TWO APPLICATIONS

2 tbsp. mashed avocado

1½ tbsp. whole wheat flour

1 tbsp. distilled water

½ tsp. jojoba oil

½ tsp. honey

You will also need: cutting board; knife; mixing spoon; fork; glass bowl; stainless steel measuring spoons

directions

1
Cut open avocado and scoop out 2 tablespoons. Place in bowl and mash with fork.

2
Mix in flour, oil, and honey. Add water. If mixture is too wet, add more flour; too dry, more water.

3
Apply to face. Avoid eye area. Leave on for 20 minutes.

4
Rinse with warm water. Pat face dry.

Mask for oily or acne-prone skin

ingredients

YIELD: ONE TO TWO APPLICATIONS

1 tbsp. whole wheat flour

1½ tbsp. green clay

1½ tbsp. apple cider vinegar

2 tbsp. witch hazel

¼ tsp. vitamin E oil

3 drops grapefruit essential oil*

Rubbing alcohol

*Caution: *Before using an essential oil, be sure to follow the health cautions contained on the copyright page iv.*

You will also need: glass bowl; stainless steel measuring spoons; spoon; eyedropper

directions

1
Combine all ingredients in bowl and stir.

2
If mixture is too wet, add more flour; too dry, more witch hazel. Clean eyedropper with rubbing alcohol to remove the oil.

3
Apply to face. Avoid eye area. Leave on for 20 minutes.

4
Rinse with warm water. Pat face dry.

97

Labels

CREATING YOUR OWN labels can be as personal as designing a beautiful greeting card. By combining fine reproduction art and an inspiring text you have composed yourself, you will be able to decorate your bottles with labels that identify their preparations. Illustrations are as nearby as your antique or old print and book stores, or perhaps in your drawers, where you may keep old postcards, greeting cards, gift wrap, even handwritten notes and letters of sentimental meaning.

Self-adhesive film

materials

Chosen container

Black-and-white line art, typeface, or full-color illustration

8½ × 11–inch clear matte or white paper adhesive film

Two-sided satin ribbon, ⅜ in. or ⅛ in. wide

You will also need: grid ruler; self-healing mat; X-Acto knife

directions

1 Follow Steps 1 and 2 of the directions on the facing page.

2 When you are satisfied with the images, arrange them on a sheet of plain 8 ½ × 11–inch paper and photocopy them onto the film.

3 Use an X-Acto knife, grid ruler, and self-healing mat to cut out individual labels; or use scissors to cut around contours for a die-cut style, being careful not to cut into the design.

4 To affix a label to a container, pull away the backing, position the image, and press the label onto container where desired.

5 To decorate the container with ribbon, cut and tie ribbon in a bow around the neck, or cut and glue pieces of ribbon to form a frame around the label.

Decoupage with ribbon tie

Note: You will need access to a color or plain paper copier for the following treatments.

materials

Chosen container

Line art or full-color illustration

ModPodge™ decoupage glue

½ yd. sheer ribbon, ¾ in. wide

Sponge brush, ½ in. wide

Optional

Sealing wax stick in gold, burgundy, or as desired

Matches

Embossing seal

Olive oil

You will also need: scissors or X-Acto knife and ruler; wax paper; cloth

directions

1
Bring your container and chosen art to a copy store.

2
Copy the image onto plain paper, reducing and enlarging, as desired.

3
When you are satisfied, photocopy your image in color or black and white.

4
Cut around the contour of the art, being careful not to cut into the lines of the design.

5
To protect the label, lay it face up on wax paper and apply a thin coat of ModPodge™; let it dry 20 minutes; repeat.

6
To decorate your container, affix the ribbon on it, positioning the midpoint of the ribbon under the base, pulling streamers taut, and tying a knot, then a bow at the top of the cap.

7
To affix the label over the ribbon, use a brush to apply ModPodge™ to the back and edges of the label, then center it over the ribbon, as shown on page 78.

8
Work any excess glue out from under the label, wiping it with a damp cloth.

9
Optional: To apply a wax seal to the label, light a wax stick and allow drops of wax to fall on the ribbon until you have a circle approximately ⅝ inch in diameter. Immediately press the embossing seal lightly coated with oil into the wax; let the wax cool and harden.

99

Eucalyptus and rose garland

THE SENSUAL PERFUME of roses and the invigorating fragrance of eucalyptus of this lush boa can transform a quick shower into an invigorating sensory experience. The rushing hot waters will change into steam and pleasantly and effectively carry the scent of these plants into the surrounding air.

Foremost, you will smell the penetrating fragrance of the eucalyptus leaves when you take a deep breath. The scent will be strong at first, then it will dissipate. This garland can be used in the bath as well, positioned around the rim of the tub if you desire. Otherwise, after you have used it in your sanctuary, you can move it to any other area in your home.

materials

Fresh plant material:

12 branches white mallee eucalyptus

18 pink roses

Medium-gauge spool wire painted green

18 plastic orchid vials

Laundry rope, approximately ⅜ in. diameter

You will also need: pruning shears; wire cutters

directions

1 Lay the branches of eucalyptus on a protected work surface.

2 Use pruning shears to cut 8 to 10 leafy sprigs from a branch, each measuring 6 to 8 inches.

3 Repeat Step 2, reserving 2 branches for center bouquets.

4 To make one bouquet, hold 5 to 7 leafy sprigs, binding their stems together with spool wire.

5 Cut the spool wire and set the bouquet aside.

6 Repeat Step 4 to make approximately 16 bouquets from the remaining sprigs.

7 Cut 16 to 20 leafy sprigs, each measuring 4 to 6 inches, from the reserved branches.

8 To make 4 center bouquets, repeat Steps 4 and 5.

9 To prepare the base of the garland, pull off and cut 5 feet of rope knotting each end in a double knot.

10 To bind the bouquets to the base, lay the head of one bouquet on the end of the rope, leaves facing and covering the knot.

11 To bind the bouquet in place, wrap spool wire around the stems; do not cut the wire.

12 Lay the head of the next bouquet over the stems of the first, binding it in place with spool wire.

13 Continue positioning and binding bouquets to create full, lush foliage, stopping at the midpoint of the base; then work from the opposite end repeating Steps 10 through 13, to the midpoint.

14 Bind the reserved bouquets to the center of the garland, concealing all exposed wire or sparseness.

15 Trim the stems of the roses on the diagonal to 5 inches.

16 Fill the orchid vials with water and secure their caps.

17 Insert the stem of a rose into the hole in a cap and set it aside.

18 Repeat Step 17 for the remaining roses.

19 Push single vials between bouquets of eucalyptus, distributing as desired.

20 Display, as desired.

101

In closing

In deep silence we return to the

ultimate cause, pure Being.

There you come face-to-face with the womb of creation,

the source of all that was, is, or will be,

which is simply yourself.

—M. Scott Peck

THE FAUCET HAS BEEN turned firmly to stop the rush of water, which now swirls like a liquid pinwheel down the drain. Vaporous curls of soft mist hover near the ceiling like small clouds, reacting to the infusion of cooler air from the slightly open door. And as you begin to dress to leave your private world, your personal sanctuary, you feel restored and revitalized. But it is not just your body that feels renewed; no, this restoration, this revitalization has occurred simultaneously on a far deeper level, as if some thread has reknit itself, as if some new connection has grown stronger. And it has. Unbidden maybe, unexpected perhaps, these gifts from your time in this quiet and soothing corner of your home are the graces that come from being in your own good company.

And so you find after all that it is enough only that you take the journey into this private room and tend to the rituals there; your spirit will carry you the rest of the way to an inner room, where you rediscover your light within. This is true. This has always been true. And when you go out into the world, the experience will go with you to meet every new day. And after a while you will see this journey to and in your personal sanctuary as a necessity of life, and you will plan carefully to reinstate it as often as possible. For in this deep place you have become aware of what your inner life is truly about, and now you can only live a life of congruence. It is from this congruence that authenticity and joy spring. *That* is the life truly lived.

Index to base oils

Here are descriptions of the base or carrier oils we have used in our preparations, along with some of their key characteristics. It is interesting to note that the oils closest to our own body oils are generally those extracted from fruits, grains, seeds and nuts. When you make your choice, consider oils that are cold-pressed or expeller-pressed because they are mechanically pressed, have had less exposure to heat, and retain more of their nutritious properties. Products that contain synthetic oils, mineral oil, or petroleum do not allow skin to breathe and so do not nourish the skin like the listed base oils. And, one important note of caution: oils can become rancid if exposed to heat and light, so it is best to purchase and use smaller quantities and store them in a cool, dark place, such as your refrigerator.

Almond Oil

Pressed from almonds, this oil is a general all-purpose oil. It is very light and virtually odorless. It can be drying, so it is best combined with heavier oils.

Avocado Oil

Derived from the flesh of the avocado, this is a rich, emollient oil that is best combined with lighter base oils. It also has antioxidant properties.

Apricot Kernel Oil

Made from the kernels of apricots, this oil is light and odorless, and can have a drying effect. It is most effective when combined with heavier oils.

Canola Oil

Made from the seeds of the rape plant, this oil is light and good for most skin types. It works best when combined with a more emollient oil, like avocado oil.

Grape Seed Oil

Pressed from the seeds of grapes, this lightest and least greasy of all the oils can be drying. It is more effective and balanced when combined with heavier oils.

Jojoba Oil

Extracted from the leaves of a small desert shrub, this oil is technically a liquid wax that closely resembles our skin's natural protective oils. It is effective in moisturizing dry or damaged skin, and has antioxidant properties.

Olive Oil

Pressed from olives, this oil is emollient, very fragrant, and stable (it will not easily go rancid). Because it is so heavy and fragrant, it is best combined with almond or apricot kernel oil to lighten it.

Sesame Oil

Derived from sesame seeds, this is a heavier oil with a strong aroma and is slightly drying. It has natural antioxidants and natural sunscreen properties.

Vitamin E Oil

Good when used alone or in combination with almond or jojoba oils, this oil. Use only 100 percent natural d–alpha tocopherol; other forms are synthetic.

Wheat Germ Oil

Extracted from the germ of the wheat kernel, this is a very strong-smelling, heavy, rich oil. It is extremely nourishing and should be used only in small quantities.

Essential oils

ESSENTIAL OILS ARE actually highly concentrated plant extracts with distinct aromatherapeutic properties that can influence your mental and physical well-being. When choosing your essential oil, consider both the fragrance and the benefit you wish to gain. Keep in mind that when blending your own oils certain ones are stronger than others and therefore you will not need as much.

Caution: *Be aware that essential oils are potent and that there are sensitivities and toxicities associated with their use, especially for pregnant women, children and the elderly. First read the warnings on copyright page iv before preparing or using essential oils and strictly follow the cautions.*

Anise: sweet, licorice, warming, clarifying; good for digestion and is head clearing.

Basil: sweet, floral, spicy, uplifting, refreshing; good for concentration and alleviates nervousness.

Bergamot: refreshing, uplifting, antiseptic, clarifying; good to relieve anxiety, depression and insomnia.

Cedarwood: woodsy, calming, soothing, harmonizing; good for building confidence.

Chamomile: relaxing, calming, soothing, anti-inflammatory; good for insomnia, alleviates anger and balances the female system and good for digestion.

Clary sage: warming, relaxing, uplifting, calming; helps alleviate depression and counters insomnia.

Clove: spicy, sweet, warming, antiseptic; good for respiratory and digestive systems.

Cinnamon: sweet, spicy, soothing, warming, antiseptic; good for digestion and respiratory system and acts as an aphrodisiac.

Cypress: woodsy, relaxing, refreshing; helps clear head and good for circulatory system.

Eucalyptus: stimulating, uplifting, antiseptic, antimicrobial, cooling, invigorating; good decongestive.

Fennel: spicy, sweet, invigorating; good muscle relaxant.

Frankincense: relaxing, rejuvenating, eases breathing; creates confidence.

Geranium: sweet, floral, refreshing, relaxing, balancing; helps anti-depressive and acts as anti-inflammatory.

Ginger: warm, spicy; acts as an anti-inflammatory and good for digestion.

Grapefruit: refreshing, invigorating, stimulating; good for creating euphoria.

Jasmine: sweet, floral, relaxing, soothing, confidence building; good for stimulating sensuality and good for the female system.

Juniper: refreshing, balancing, relaxing; good for relaxing muscles and stimulates appetite.

Lavender: clean, sweet, floral, relaxing, calming, soothing; acts as muscle relaxant and anti-depressant, and counters insomnia.

Lemon: tangy, cooling, refreshing, stimulating, uplifting, astringent, antiseptic; good for circulatory system and helps focus concentration and sharpens senses.

Lemongrass: antiseptic, astringent, toning, refreshing; acts as antiseptic and astringent.

Marjoram: warming, sedating, calming, relaxing; good muscle relaxant.

Melissa: calming, antiseptic, refreshing; acts as anti-depressant.

Myrrh: sweet, strengthening, rejuvenating; acts as anti-inflammatory, helps digestive and respiratory systems.

Neroli: relaxing, antibacterial, calming, dispels fears; helps heal the skin and can be used as anti-depressant.

Orange: sweet, refreshing, relaxing; good antiseptic.

Patchouli: rich, spicy, woodsy, relaxing; helps alleviate depression and acts as aphrodisiac.

Peppermint: stimulating, refreshing, invigorating, cooling; acts as muscle relaxant, good for indigestion and for balancing the female system.

Rose: sweet, floral, relaxing, soothing, sensual; uplifts emotions and helps alleviate irritability, stress and anger.

Rosemary: antiseptic, invigorating, refreshing, stimulating; stimulates circulation and good for circulatory system and, for memory and concentration.

Sage: fresh, invigorating, astringent, stimulating; good to relieve sore muscles, acts as antiseptic.

Sandalwood: exotic, sweet, woodsy, relaxing, warming, grounding; helps relieve stress, good for balance, confidence and in general, for nervous system.

Tea Tree: clean, spicy, antiseptic, antifungal, invigorating; good decongestive, and helps respiratory system.

Thyme: antiseptic, refreshing, stimulating; good muscle relaxant, good for circulatory and respiratory system.

Vanilla: sweet, warming, sensual, soothing; acts as aphrodisiac.

Ylang ylang: exotic, floral, relaxing, soothing, sensual; helps to alleviate anger and irritability and acts as aphrodisiac.

Patterns

Sources

THE FOLLOWING LIST includes stores that carry a wide line of bath products and accessories. For specific information and the location of a store near you, call the telephone number listed.

ABC Carpet
888 Broadway
New York, NY 10003
212-473-3000

Bath and Body Works
800-395-1001

Bed, Bath and Beyond
212-255-3550
516-420-7050

Bergdorf Goodman
754 Fifth Avenue
New York, NY 10019
212-753-7300

Bloomingdale's
212-355-5900
800-777-4999 [catalog]

The Body Shop
800-541-2535

Chambers
800-334-9890 [catalog]

Crate & Barrel
800-323-5461

Garden Botanika
800-877-9603 [for West Coast]

H2O+
800-242-BATH

Hold Everything
800-421-2264

IKEA
800-434-4532 [catalog]

Kiehl's
800-KIEHLS-1

Léron
750 Madison Avenue
New York, NY 10021
212-753-6700

Origins
800-723-7310

Pier 1
800-447-4371

Portico
139 Spring Street
New York, NY 10012
212-941-7722

Pottery Barn
800-922-5507 [catalog]

Restoration Hardware
800-762-1005 [catalog]

Saks Fifth Avenue
212-753-4000

Takashimaya
800-753-2038

Waterworks
469 Broome Street
New York, NY 10013
212-966-6747

Bibliography

Allardice, Pamela. *The Art of Aromatherapy: A Guide to Using Essential Oils for Health and Relaxation*. New York: Random House, 1998.

Breedlove, Greta. *The Herbal Home Spa: Naturally Refreshing Wraps, Rubs, Lotions, Masks, Oils, and Scrubs*. Vermont: Storey Books, 1998.

Calbom, Cherie, and Maureen Keane. *Juicing for Life*. Garden City Park, NY: Avery Publishing Group, 1992.

Chopra, Deepak. *The Way of the Wizard: Twenty Spiritual Lessons in Creating the Life You Want*. New York: Harmony Books, 1995.

Crawford, Ilse. *The Sensual Home: Liberate Your Senses and Change Your Life*. New York: Rizzoli, 1997.

Estes, Clarissa Pinkola. *Women Who Run with the Wolves: Myths and Stories of the Wild Woman Archetype*. New York: Ballantine Books, 1992.

Falconi, Dina. *Earthly Bodies and Heavenly Hair: Natural and Healthy Personal Care for Every Body*. Woodstock, NY: Ceres Press, 1998.

Golden, Manine Rosa. *Home Spa at Pier 1*. New York: Abbeville Press, 1997.

Harrar, Sari and Sara Altshul O'Donnell. *The Woman's Book of Healing Herbs*, Prevention Health Books for Women.

Moore, Thomas. *Care of the Soul: A Guide for Cultivating Depth and Sacredness in Everyday Life*. New York: HarperCollins, 1992.

Nixon, Deborah. *The Practical Art of Aromatherapy: Create Your Own Personalized Beauty Treatments and Natural Remedies*. New York: Random House, 1998.

Peck, M. Scott. *The Road Less Traveled: A New Psychology of Love, Traditional Values, and Spiritual Growth*. New York: Simon & Schuster, 1978.

Saeks, Diane Dorrans. *Bathrooms*. San Francisco: Chronicle Books, 1998.

Slavin, Sara, and Karl Petzke. *The Art of the Bath*. San Francisco: Chronicle Books, 1997.

Stone, Jeff, and Kim Johnson Gross. *Bath*. New York: Alfred A. Knopf, 1993.

Van Steenhouse, Andrea, and Doris A. Fuller. *A Woman's Guide to a Simpler Life*. New York: Harmony Books, 1996.

Vara, Jon, and editors of *The Old Farmer's Almanac. Home Wisdom: A Commonsense Guide to Solving Everyday Problems*. New York: Time-Life Books, 1997.

Von Furstenberg, Diane. *The Bath*. New York: Random House, 1993.

Index